Detroit Free Press

BIG BLUE

MICHIGAN'S DOMINANT 2026 CHAMPIONSHIP SEASON

JASON LACOSS/INDYSTAR

SHOCK THE WORLD
BOYS
GO BLUE !
CHAMPS
CHAMP
CHAMPIONS

JUNFU HAN/DETROIT FREE PRESS

THE LINEUP

Book editor
Gene Myers

Sports editor
Ryan Ford

Assistant sports editors
Marlowe Alter
Andrew Birkle

Free Press editor
Nicole Avery Nichols

Beat reporter
Tony Garcia

Columnists
Mitch Albom
Carlos Monarrez
Shawn Windsor

Photographers
Junfu Han
Eric Seals

Proofreader
Sherrill Amo

Project coordinator
Gene Myers

Special thanks
Alicia Del Gallo
Chris Thomas
Noah Amstadter
Josh Williams
Clarissa Young
Clarissa Shine
Jared Sábado-Hernández

Content packaged by Mojo Media, Inc.
Joe Funk
Jason Hinman

CHRISTINE TANNOUS/INDYSTAR

ABOUT THE BOOK: *Big Blue* condenses a year's worth of the world's best coverage of the Michigan Wolverines from the Detroit Free Press. For continuing coverage of the Wolverines, go to freep.com. Order print and digital subscriptions or access the eNewspaper at subscribe.freep.com/offers. This book includes coverage from the USA TODAY Network, which includes the Free Press.

Double the glory: Limited copies remain of *Blue Reign!* – the Detroit Free Press book that chronicled the Wolverines' march to the 2023 College Football Playoff championship. It retails for $16.95, plus shipping and tax. Order at triumphbooks.com/MichiganWin.

Detroit Free Press | 

Front and back cover photos by JUNFU HAN/DETROIT FREE PRESS

PRINTED IN U.S.A.
ISBN: 979-8-89855-019-6

This is an unofficial publication. This book is in no way affiliated with, licensed by or endorsed by the NCAA or the University of Michigan.

TRIUMPHBOOKS.COM
@TRIUMPHBOOKS

814 North Franklin Street
Chicago, Illinois 60610
Phone: (312) 337-0747

BIG BLUE

JUNFU HAN/DETROIT FREE PRESS

10

THE CHAMPS

Two seasons after going 8-24, the Michigan Wolverines stormed to a 37-3 record and captured their second national championship, beating UConn in the title game.

18

THE SEASON

Riding a dominant frontcourt, the Wolverines reached No. 1 in the polls twice, defeated Michigan State twice and coasted to the Big Ten title with a 19-1 record.

66

THE GLORY

The No. 1 seed in the Midwest, the Wolverines steamrolled their way through stops in Buffalo and Chicago before cutting down the nets in Indianapolis.

WERNER

INTRODUCTION

The greatest basketball team at Michigan? Hail, yes!

By Shawn Windsor | April 6, 2026

The Michigan Wolverines are national title winners for the second time in their history after beating Connecticut in the championship game. This book is the story of how the best basketball team in school history blasted its way through the season and the Men's NCAA Tournament.

The team came together in a hurry, transfers joining high school recruits, and the veteran holdovers joining both. Coach Dusty May showed how to build chemistry and camaraderie in short order and reminded everyone that when players feel connected and part of something larger, it didn't matter how long they had been together.

The Wolverines knew they had the makings of something special from the beginning, almost from the moment they all got in the gym. That was back in the summer, when the coaches looked at each other as the players flowed up and down the court. They knew then, despite all the new faces, that they had the makings of something special.

Good enough to play on the final Monday night of the season, their coach said back when camp began in the fall. He wasn't shy about how good his Michigan Wolverines could be.

They started slowly, needing overtime to beat Wake Forest in Detroit and the full 40 minutes to beat Texas Christian in Fort Worth. Then the Wolverines took a trip out to the desert during Thanksgiving week.

Three nights in Las Vegas changed everything.

Michigan thumped San Diego State by 40 points in The Players Era Festival and followed that with a 30-point victory over No. 25 Auburn and a 40-point victory over No. 10 Gonzaga. The Wolverines had averaged 99 points a game; their average margin of victory was 36.7 points.

They shot up the polls and grabbed the attention of the college basketball world.

Suddenly, the words of star forward Yaxel Lendeborg didn't seem so outlandish. By the time the Wolverines demoralized No. 7 Purdue at Mackey Arena, one of the toughest places to play in America, the irrepressible UAB transfer sounded prophetic:

"We continue to think we're the best team ever assembled."

May loved the confidence, even welcomed it because he knew how much his players liked playing for one another, and that Lendeborg hadn't said those words to seek attention. He believed them. And his teammates believed in him, the future All-American and Big Ten player of the year who loved to pass.

Every one of these Wolverines loved to pass, defend and give up a good shot in search of a great one. It was beautiful and thrilling all at once, and it's the story of the most dominant Michigan basketball team in history.

Enjoy. ■

Homegrown Michigan guard Trey McKenny and the Wolverines captured the program's first title since 1989. JUNFU HAN/DETROIT FREE PRESS

MICHIGAN'S NATIONAL CHAMPIONSHIP
2025-26 SEASON SUMMARY

RECORD
37-3

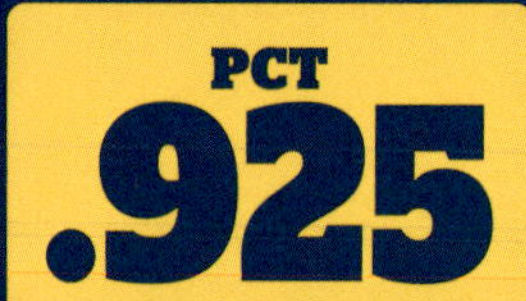
PCT
.925

REGULAR SEASON

Nov. 3, 2025 | W | 121-78
VS. OAKLAND

Nov. 11, 2025 | W | 85-84 (OT)
WAKE FOREST

Nov. 14, 2025 | W | 67-63
AT TCU

Nov. 19, 2025 | W | 86-61
VS. MIDDLE TENNESSEE

Nov. 24, 2025 | W | 94-54
SAN DIEGO STATE

Nov. 25, 2025 | W | 102-72
NO. 25 AUBURN

Nov. 26, 2025 | W | 101-61
NO. 10 GONZAGA

Dec. 6, 2025 | W | 101-60
VS. RUTGERS

Dec. 9, 2025 | W | 89-61
VS. VILLANOVA

Dec. 13, 2025 | W | 101-83
AT MARYLAND

Dec. 21, 2025 | W | 102-50
VS. LA SALLE

Dec. 29, 2025 | W | 112-71
VS. McNEESE

Jan. 2, 2026 | W | 96-66
VS. USC

Jan. 6, 2026 | W | 74-72
AT PENN STATE

Jan. 10, 2026 | L | 91-88
VS. WISCONSIN

Jan. 14, 2026 | W | 82-72
AT WASHINGTON

Jan. 17, 2026 | W | 81-71
AT OREGON

Jan. 20, 2026 | W | 86-72
VS. INDIANA

Jan. 23, 2026 | **W** | **74-62**
VS. OHIO STATE

Jan. 27, 2026 | **W** | **75-72**
VS. NO. 5 NEBRASKA

Jan. 30, 2026 | **W** | **83-71**
AT NO. 8 MICHIGAN STATE

FEB. 5, 2026 | **W** | **110-69**
VS. PENN STATE

FEB. 8, 2026 | **W** | **82-61**
AT OHIO STATE

FEB. 11, 2026 | **W** | **87-75**
AT NORTHWESTERN

FEB. 14, 2026 | **W** | **86-56**
VS. UCLA

FEB. 17, 2026 | **W** | **91-80**
AT NO. 7 PURDUE

FEB. 21, 2026 | **L** | **68-63**
NO. 3 DUKE

FEB. 24, 2026 | **W** | **77-67**
VS. MINNESOTA

FEB. 27, 2026 | **W** | **84-70**
AT NO. 11 ILLINOIS

MARCH 5, 2026 | **W** | **71-68**
AT IOWA

MARCH 8, 2026 | **W** | **90-80**
VS. NO. 8 MICHIGAN STATE

BIG TEN TOURNAMENT

MARCH 13, 2026 | **W** | 71-67
OHIO STATE

MARCH 14, 2026 | **W** | 68-65
NO. 23 WISCONSIN

MARCH 15, 2026 | **L** | 80-72
NO. 18 PURDUE

NCAA TOURNAMENT

MARCH 19, 2026 | **W** | 101-80
NO. 16 HOWARD

MARCH 21, 2026 | **W** | 95-72
NO. 9 SAINT LOUIS

MARCH 27, 2026 | **W** | 90-77
NO. 4 ALABAMA

MARCH 29, 2026 | **W** | 95-62
NO. 6 TENNESSEE

APRIL 4, 2026 | **W** | 91-73
NO. 1 ARIZONA

APRIL 6, 2026 | **W** | **69-63**
NO. 2 UCONN

THE CHAMPS

JUNFU HAN/DETROIT FREE PRESS

MOUNTAINTOP

In basketball's new era, Michigan wins it all with old-fashioned grit

By Mitch Albom | April 6, 2026

Long after the buzzer had sounded, even when half of Lucas Oil Stadium already had cleared out, the Michigan basketball team still wouldn't leave the court, which at the Final Four is elevated like a stage, a fitting platform for the drama the Wolverines had just performed.

Yaxel Lendeborg kept hugging people. Elliot Cadeau smiled for the TV cameras. Aday Mara draped himself in a Spanish flag.

Finally, with pieces of net in their hair, championship caps on their heads, and the sweet sweat of victory drying on their skin, the players and coaches headed to the locker room through a massive cheering section, which burst into a chant that echoed to the rafters:

"IT'S GREAT ... TO BE ... A MICH-I-GAN WOL-VER-INE!"

Hard to argue. With a scrappy, herky-jerky 69-63 victory over a relentless Connecticut team, Michigan captured its second national basketball title, 37 years after its first, easing the sting of four previous trips to the mountaintop that ended empty-handed.

It was hardly easy. In fact, for much of the night, it was like that dream where you're giving a speech without your clothes on. Everything the Wolverines normally did, they weren't doing. Their best player was a shadow. Their long shots were clanking. They had almost no assists. They were getting outrebounded.

But it's a trademark of this gifted and now legendary group that when the rabbit won't come out of the hat, they just find another rabbit. Can't make shots? Block them. Can't get assists? Steal the ball. Can't find your rhythm? Squeeze the Huskies off theirs. This game was like watching two movie combatants wrestle each other into the ocean: messy and gasping, but if we're going under, so are you.

And only one of us is coming back up.

Blue survives.

Down comes the net.

"How will you want this team to be remembered?" a TV reporter asked Lendeborg, the Big Ten player of the year, in the immediate aftermath of this crazy U-M victory, which capped a record-setting 37-3 season with a championship cherry on top.

"They may call us mercenaries," Lendeborg replied, "but we're the hardest-playing team in college basketball! And the best team in college basketball!"

It's great to be a Wolverine.

A dance in Connecticut mud

Let's say it right now. This is a new era in college hoops and a new way of doing things in Ann Arbor — and most everywhere else. Here was the first team to win an NCAA title starting five transfer players. And it won't be the last. There's no telling how many Wolverines will be coming back from this group. But

Coach Dusty May cut down national championship nets two years after taking over an 8-24 program. JUNFU HAN/DETROIT FREE PRESS

CHAMPIONS
M
WERNER

then, that's pretty much the mantra everywhere in this sport right now.

What we do know is that coach Dusty May, in just his second year, molded a group of newcomers into a tightly knit, family-style unit, one that truly doesn't care who gets the big numbers or the final shot, as long as it results in a victory. If it's alchemy, then he's a wizard. Remember, many of Michigan's "stars" were riding benches with their previous teams last year.

In nine months, they became a unit that cried not at winning the title, but at their final practice. A group that enjoyed when May brought baskets into Michigan Stadium last week so that they could simulate what shooting in a football stadium would be like.

That kind of chemistry is a credit to May and his staff. You don't win a game like Monday night's — one where everything looks upside down — if you haven't drilled your players until confidence is second nature, and backup plans can be implemented as easily as sliding open another drawer.

"All year we've been finding ways to win," said Cadeau, the mop-top point guard who won the Final Four most outstanding player award after leading the way Monday night with 19 points and an almost uncountable tally of fouls drawn from UConn players. "We made two 3s the whole game. We weren't making shots. We had a couple assists ... but we've constantly been finding ways to win all year, no matter how everybody is playing."

On Monday, they needed to. The first half was played in Connecticut mud. After an early Wolverines spurt, the Huskies began taking it to Michigan the way quicksand takes to a body. Slog, slog. Erase your speed. Slog, slog. Outhustle you for rebounds. Slog, slog. The more you press, the more uncomfortable things get.

It worked — for a bit. Michigan was a mess. Here was Lendeborg, clearly in pain from ankle and knee injuries, being little more than a toll booth — one basket, no rebounds and no assists in the first 20 minutes. Here was Mara missing his first three looks, losing his dominance off the boards. Here was Cadeau, after some early fireworks, saddled with two fouls and sitting on the bench, watching his teammates look discombobulated on offense.

Here were the high-scoring Wolverines — who racked up more than 90 points in each of their previous five games in this tournament — missing all eight of their 3-point shots in that first half, getting no fast-break baskets (except a hard put-back rebound) and barely cracking 30 points before halftime. Their previous low for a half in this Big Dance had been 47.

A TV reporter asked UConn coach Dan Hurley about the pace his team was imposing.

"We're dragging them into probably the only kind of game that we have a chance to win," he said.

Mud's the word.

Old champ recognizing new champ

And yet, somehow Michigan came into halftime with a four-point lead. Then — and this is likely where the game was won — they regrouped.

"Early in the second half the game got a little bit chippy and physical, so we thought, this is going to be a game we just have to figure it out," May said. "We did feel like we were defending well enough that we were going to be able to find enough baskets."

Using that defense — they would finish with six blocks and six steals — the Wolverines eventually edged to their biggest lead, 11 points, thanks mostly to drawing fouls and making their foul shots. They would sink more

Forward Morez Johnson Jr. put up 12 points and 10 rebounds in a very physical game against UConn. ERIC SEALS/DETROIT FREE PRESS

Wilson
NCAA
MICHIGAN
21
MULLINS
24

free throws than baskets (25 to 21) and shoot them at a much higher percentage (89.3% versus 38.2%).

But it was the timing of their moments that won the night. Whenever UConn pulled close, the Wolverines came up with a play to push the Huskies back underwater.

Here was guard Roddy Gayle Jr., when the Huskies had pulled within five points, taking a steal and lobbing a perfect pass to Mara for a wicked slam that drew a roar. Here was Cadeau, with UConn making a late surge, drawing an offensive foul, then drawing a defensive foul. Here was freshman Trey McKenney, after UConn's heart-and-soul leader, Alex Karaban, sank a huge 3-pointer to cut the deficit to six, taking the wild end of a whip-around play and calmly hitting a 3 of his own.

That basket — with less than two minutes to go — may have been the one that broke the Huskies' spirit. UConn was a team that had won two of the past three national titles. At that moment, you sensed the old champion was recognizing the new champion.

A few moments later, it became reality. The final points came off two free throws by young McKenney, just as 37 years ago, the Wolverines' first championship came off of two free throws by Rumeal Robinson.

"Everybody on this team is extremely talented," McKenney said later. "A lot of us could be somewhere else doing more than what we've done (individually) this season. But I think it just shows that this team is super-selfless. I've never been around such a talented group of guys that are willing to take a lesser role for somebody next to them."

And by taking less, they just got the most.

Down comes the net.

A magical team and season

Thus ends a season for the ages, and the dawn of what Michigan fans no doubt feel is a golden era for its basketball team. May inherited a program that had eight victories in 2023-24. He has had 64 wins in two seasons since.

But it was the way Michigan won that will be remembered when this season is done. Dominating teams on offense (like beating Gonzaga by 40) and leading the nation in all kinds of defensive categories, while also leading in strength of schedule.

That's a damn difficult daily double, and something that will be marveled at when they write the detailed history of this team.

For the moment, as with any dewy-fresh championship, it's still just snapshots. Lendeborg, who muscled through his injury, hugging his mother in the stands, after telling the TV cameras he wanted to "take care of her forever." And Cadeau, who was never quite appreciated at North Carolina, cradling the MOP trophy. And Mara, the first Spanish man to win a Final Four, answering the question "what are they thinking in Spain right now?" by saying, "I hope they are asleep."

And finally, May, the alchemist, coming off that stage and hearing that chant:

"ITS GREAT ... TO BE ... A MICH-I-GAN WOL-VER-INE!"

As he entered the tunnel, he stopped to autograph a jersey from a young fan hanging over the railing. It's nice to see that, in a moment that could have been all about him, he made it about someone else. Or maybe he just didn't want to leave the space where, after 37 years, the magic had finally happened again.

Down comes the net.

Can you blame him? ■

Roddy Gayle Jr. made only one basket – a memorable dunk over former Michigan big man Tarris Reed Jr. ERIC SEALS/DETROIT FREE PRESS

MICHIGAN
11
AL FOUR
UCONN
5
BIG EAST
LL
1
BALL

THE SEASON

JUNFU HAN/DETROIT FREE PRESS

NATTY OR BUST?

On paper, Michigan has its best team in a decade, but will it pay off?

By Tony Garcia | November 2, 2025

College basketball games aren't played on paper.

If they were, Michigan already should clear some room in its trophy case.

As constituted for the 2025-26 season, the Wolverines arguably have their most talent in the past decade — perhaps even more than when Trey Burke ran the point flanked by Nik Stauskas, Glenn Robinson III and Mitch McGary.

There will be injuries, upsets and, more than likely, a surprise team in the Big Ten. But coach Dusty May knows he has enough to make this season one to remember in Ann Arbor.

"I don't think anyone on last year's team or this year's team would disagree," May said. "We have more natural ability, more proven success on this year's team than last."

Last year's Wolverines finished second in the Big Ten during the regular season, won the Big Ten Tournament and advanced to the Sweet 16. With more talent top to bottom, four players who have a year in May's system and a coaching staff returning in full, the Wolverines' optimism is up to the rafters, where Burke's jersey will head in January.

Now, it's about May and company getting the most out of it.

Are those expectations too high?

"I don't know. Who knows? I think that's so far down the list of what we need to be concerned with right now," May said. "If you get lost in the fight, then the external expectations (could) poison the group. But that's on us to be aware, honest and accountable every single day and hopefully that's enough."

The transfer talent

As much as the Wolverines bring back experience, their title hopes start with their class of transfers — one of the top 10 in the nation, according to just about every ranking.

It starts with Yaxel Lendeborg, who U-M was able to lure away from UAB and then the NBA with the promise of a year of development. Already, he had averaged 29.5 points and 11 rebounds in two exhibition games, earned preseason All-America nods and was, by all accounts, one of the most talented players in the country.

May has been harsh about Lendeborg's practice habits, but he's a dedicated teammate and facilitator.

"My first instinct is always to pass," Lendeborg said. "Coming off a screen, I'm going to have a lot of shooters around me. I can make that pass to a shooter. ... If the opportunity for me to score is there, then I have to take that."

Elsewhere, Morez Johnson Jr. comes in from Illi-

Morez Johnson Jr. became a key piece for Michigan after transferring from conference rival Illinois. WENDELL CRUZ/IMAGN IMAGES

MICHIGAN
21
SELLERS
4
ST. JO
23
24
HYUNDAI
HARRY
STYLES

nois after he starred for Team USA's U-19 team — gold medal winners over the summer.

He dealt with a lower body injury for some of the leadup to the season, but it didn't seem to affect him in his maize-and-blue debut: 16 points, eight rebounds and two blocks in an exhibition victory over St. John's on Oct. 25 at Madison Square Garden.

That was also the night UCLA transfer Aday Mara played his first game. A 7-foot-3 tower from Spain still was working on his physicality, but his size made him a walking rim protector. He's an elite passer, too, as he put up 13 points, five rebounds, four assists and two blocks in 22 minutes against the Red Storm.

"Since I was a child and I was starting to play basketball, I always wanted to make a fancy pass," Mara said. "I really prefer to make a really good assist than make, I don't know, a basket. (Coaches) always told me that when you make an assist, it makes two people happy. If you score, it's just you."

The final addition was Elliot Cadeau, a pass-first point guard inbound from North Carolina; he finished second in the ACC in assists last season.

Cadeau gives U-M the true facilitator it lacked last season. May has encouraged him to get more active on the defensive glass so that he can grab boards, push the ball up court and distribute to the wealth of playmakers around him — or just finish at the rim.

Cadeau, a former McDonald's All-American, is expected to set the offense up for lob looks at the rim and facilitate May's attack with quick precision.

Sneaky returning talent

May called U-M's talent a "prerequisite" for success. This year will be about finding what he calls "connectors" — players who don't need the ball to impact the game, whether that's with spacing, knowledge of the system or leadership in executing the details.

The top options? Nimari Burnett, Roddy Gayle Jr. and Will Tschetter, all in their second year with May.

Burnett was the nation's most efficient shooter last year in mid-January.

"Nimari's all about the right stuff, and he's a professional," May said.

Tschetter has bought in to his role on the wing, transforming his body by losing weight and adding quick-twitch muscles under strength coach Matt Aldred.

Instead of being an undersized big, he will be an oversized three — he showed how useful that could be as U-M's lone player to score in double figures without a turnover against St. John's. He also has been U-M's vocal leader all offseason.

"Will Tschetter, to be honest, down the stretch (against St. John's), we looked like a different team when he was out there," May said. "When you have unique pieces, then you've got to find a way to connect it and make it all work together. So, yeah, those two guys certainly have to be two players that make it work."

Gayle, the former Buckeye who drew the ire of fans last season for his struggles, should have a clean slate. While working as a creator on offense, his physicality translates to defense. It's early, but he averaged 14 points during exhibition play and had the best plus-minus (+11) of anybody in New York.

That leaves L.J. Cason as an underrated X-factor and coaches expecting a sophomore surge.

The fresh faces

And then there are the new kids, ranging from McDonald's All-American Trey McKenney from Orchard Lake St. Mary's to 7-foot-1 German big Malick Kordel.

Winters Grady provides elite shooting if he can hang on defense. Oscar Goodman will be a depth piece in the frontcourt. But there's little doubt McKenney is the one coaches expect the most out of right away.

"He's just ahead of the curve: physically, high IQ, shoots the ball at an elite level, (in) all three levels," Burnett said. "You could just see that he's above, especially in a high school, that he was above in those areas, and he's going to help tremendously."

U-M has at least two players it trusts at every position. It's more athletic, has more individual playmaking and possibly better shooting than a season ago.

The Wolverines will need to cut down on the turnovers — a noted problem a year ago and a recurring issue through two October exhibitions — but that's what exhibitions are for.

May has returned the juice to the U-M program just a season after it finished in the league basement. Now, the regular-season title is the goal — with dreams of playing into April.

"Nothing less than a Final Four (will satisfy) me," Lendeborg said. "I feel like we have the team to get there, and even more." ■

BIG TEN PRESEASON POLL

In Dusty May's debut season in 2024-25, Michigan finished second in the Big Ten behind Michigan State in the regular season and beat Wisconsin in the championship game of the tournament. For 2025-26, in a preseason poll of 28 media members through the conference's coast-to-coast footprint, the Wolverines were picked to finish second again. Purdue received 25 first-place votes and U-M the other three in the poll conducted by the IndyStar and Columbus Dispatch. The order:

1. Purdue
2. **Michigan**
3. UCLA
4. Illinois
5. Oregon
6. Michigan State
7. Wisconsin
8. Iowa
9. Ohio State
10. Indiana
11. Washington
12. Southern Cal
13. Maryland
14. Nebraska
15. Northwestern
16. Minnesota
17. Rutgers
18. Penn State

MICHIGAN WOLVERINES ROSTER

NAME	NO	POS	HT	WT	CLASS	BIRTHPLACE
Nimari Burnett	4	G	6-5	195	GR	Chicago, IL
Elliot Cadeau	3	G	6-1	180	JR	West Orange, NJ
L.J. Cason	2	G	6-2	195	SO	Lakeland, FL
Howard Eisley Jr.	7	G	6-0	200	SO	New York, NY
Roddy Gayle Jr.	11	G	6-5	210	SR	Niagara Falls, NY
Oscar Goodman	5	F	6-7	235	FR	Opunake, New Zealand
Winters Grady	10	G/F	6-6	210	FR	Tualatin, OR
Harrison Hochberg	13	F	6-7	220	JR	New York, NY
Morez Johnson Jr.	21	F	6-9	250	SO	Riverdale, IL
Malick Kordel	32	C	7-2	275	FR	Oberhausen, Germany
Yaxel Lendeborg	23	F	6-9	240	GR	Pennsauken, NJ
Ricky Liburd	0	G/F	6-4	190	FR	Hollywood, FL
Aday Mara	15	C	7-3	255	JR	Zaragoza, Spain
Charlie May	12	G	6-5	190	SR	Boca Raton, FL
Trey McKenney	1	G	6-4	225	FR	Flint, MI
Will Tschetter	42	F	6-8	230	GR	Stewartville, MN

NOVEMBER 3, 2025 | ANN ARBOR. MICHIGAN
NO. 7 MICHIGAN 121, OAKLAND 78

A BANNER NIGHT

After saluting B1G tourney title, Wolverines shoot the lights out in opener

By Tony Garcia

If ever there's a time to borrow a quote from Ron Burgundy in "Anchorman," it's right now.

"Boy, that escalated quickly. ... I mean that really got out of hand fast."

Michigan got out of hand in its season opener as it made its first seven shots, set a school record with 69 points in the first half and tied a school record with 19 made 3-pointers in a 121-78 destruction of Oakland at Crisler Center.

The Wolverines raised a banner for their 2025 Big Ten Tournament title before the opening tip, and they played like a team capable of raising much more than that in 2026 in front of an energized home crowd.

"I do think it's reassuring that people outside of your locker room believe in your guys," coach Dusty May said. "If we're going to be there in late March, early April, we're going to have to have incredible practice habits today, so we'll use it in a positive manner.

"We're definitely not going to raise a banner for preseason Final Four, but it's great for recruiting, great for our fan base. ... I'm all for it, but it doesn't mean anything."

What does mean something is what the Wolverines looked like. There may not be a cleaner game U-M plays all season, and it's worth noting they were far from full strength.

Superstar transfer Yaxel Lendeborg hadn't practiced in some time and played essentially left-handed with a heavy bandage on his right (shooting) hand and wrist. Sophomore guard L.J. Cason could have played but didn't have his wind back after sitting out time with an injury. And Winters Grady missed the contest in a walking boot, but he is expected to practice later this week.

Despite missing pieces, the Wolverines looked like a well-oiled machine. U-M had 29 assists, seven players scored in double figures and the Wolverines shot better than 64% from the floor, 54% from long range and missed only 1 of 13 free throws.

It won bench points (55-7), rebounds (40-22), points off turnovers (19-4), points in the paint (46-26) and points on the fast break (10-6). U-M needed 13 seconds to take the lead as it made 13 of its first 16 shots and never missed more than two shots in a row all night.

"I would tell you that was one of the best performances I've ever seen a team play in early November," said Oakland's Greg Kampe, a coach for more than four decades. "For early November, I was pretty amazed."

Transfer Morez Johnson Jr. paced the Wolverines with 24 points, but after the game May cited his "invisible" plays as much as his final line — calling him a "junkyard dog."

Freshman Trey McKenney also stood out, knocking down 6 of 8 3-pointers and scoring 21 points. Not bad after shooting 1 of 10 in two exhibitions.

"This team is deep," he said. "And everybody didn't even play. This is going to be a really good team."

Freshman Trey McKenney, Michigan's Mr. Basketball in 2025, scored 21 points in his debut. JUNFU HAN/DETROIT FREE PRESS

He pointed out the starter-caliber players on the bench, such as Will Tschetter, who scored 16. Meanwhile, Lendeborg came off the bench, adding 12 points without missing a shot.

Nimari Burnett made his standard four long balls for 14 points. Roddy Gayle Jr. had a quiet 11, and Aday Mara had a double-double with 11 points and 10 rebounds. The man who stirred the drink all night was Elliot Cadeau, who May called a "true point guard" after he recorded 12 assists, the most by a U-M player in four years.

It's exactly what May told his team it would need to be in order to have a special season.

"Ton of fun," Tschetter said. "Everybody contributing, everyone playing unselfish."

There were moments all night that May had to be proud of, but the one that may have tickled his fancy the most he wasn't even present for. Tschetter was asked about what it's like to score 121 points in a game — tied for the fifth most in U-M history — and he said that the defense left a lot "to be desired."

The group set a goal at halftime to hold Oakland to under 60 points but "didn't even come close." ▪

NOVEMBER 11, 2025 | DETROIT, MICHIGAN
NO. 5 MICHIGAN 85, WAKE FOREST 84 (OT)

A+ NIGHT FOR ADAY

7-foot-3 Mara terrorizes Demon Deacons on offense and defense

By Tony Garcia

The tallest man on the court made the biggest impact on the game.

Not only did 7-foot-3 center Aday Mara have the best statistical performance with 18 points, 14 rebounds, six assists and five blocks, but he made the difference in crunch time at Little Caesars Arena.

Wake Forest had the ball down by one point with 6.6 seconds left in overtime when Nate Calmese got it at the left wing, slashed through the lane and sent a high-arching shot at the rim over Mara.

The threat of his presence altered the shot just enough to force Calmese to change the angle and the ball caromed off the glass, then the rim and fell harmlessly to the floor as Michigan survived 85-84 in overtime. Elliot Cadeau, U-M's point guard who also had 18 points to go with seven boards and six assists, knows exactly what that feels like.

"He alters basically every shot at the rim," Cadeau said. "It's been a struggle for me to get used to that in practice. ... You see how high the kid had to throw the ball in the air not to get blocked, and that's a really hard shot to make."

Mara, who spent the past two years at UCLA, had never played more than 30 minutes in a game. On this Tuesday night in downtown Detroit, he played 37.

Michigan preached in the offseason about how a key part of its attack would be lobs to the rim. Consider the first play of overtime as Exhibit A, where Mara caught an alley-oop from Cadeau and threw it down to take the lead.

That was the most important of the bunch, but he'd been doing it all night. Mara caught passes by the rim from Cadeau, Will Tschetter and L.J. Cason and finished each with authority.

He did the same off a Roddy Gayle Jr. miss as well as one by Morez Johnson Jr. While Mara is slender and still susceptible to getting pushed off his spots, when he gets the ball that close to the rim it's game over.

"Get badminton (rackets) out." Wake Forest coach Steve Forbes said. "You can't emulate that in practice. You can't really tell how tall he is until you walk out there. That's why I didn't come out for warm-ups. I didn't want to see him."

Of Mara's 14 rebounds, five were offensive rebounds, which helped him make 8 of 11 shots.

Mara grinned when asked about how seemingly every time he grabbed a defensive rebound, his eyes immediately went up court and he looked to heave it down court.

The reason it looked like that? It's what was going through his head. He even connected on a few, like the pass to Yaxel Lendeborg, who dashed up the right side of the court and threw down a slam to tie the game at 18.

"I used to do that when I was a kid," Mara said.

Center Aday Mara was a big addition – literally and figuratively – as a transfer from UCLA. JUNFU HAN/DETROIT FREE PRESS

He had been billed as an elite passer for a big man, and it was on display. He had a touch pass to Johnson in the second half not long before he saw over the defense and whipped a two-hand pass to a cutting Trey McKenney, who finished a reverse layup. Moments later, Mara was on the facilitating end of an alley-oop to Lendeborg for a 66-64 lead.

Mara's six assists were second only to Cadeau's seven.

For every play he made on offense, there was one to match on defense. Mara recorded five blocks, but that might be corrected closer to six or seven.

Twice late in regulation he denied layup attempts as the Demon Deacons were looking to retake the lead.

"I'm always trying to tell my teammates, 'Just don't foul when someone goes to the paint," Mara said. "Because I'm always trying to block the ball. I prefer not letting in layups." ■

PLAYERS ERA FESTIVAL CHAMPIONSHIP

NOVEMBER 26, 2025 | LAS VEGAS, NEVADA

NO. 6 MICHIGAN 101, NO. 10 GONZAGA 61

VIVA LAS VEGAS

Wolverines rout three good teams by a combined 110 points

By Tony Garcia

Michigan went out to Las Vegas and hit the jackpot:

Three blowouts in three nights and a $1 million NIL bonus prize to split amongst the team.

And in the championship game of the Players Era Festival, the sixth-ranked Wolverines obliterated 10th-ranked Gonzaga 101-61.

The finale was billed as a heavyweight matchup in every regard — the 90.3 "thrill score" from KenPom was the highest in the site's history for a nonconference game — and coach Dusty May's team made it look like a buy game.

On the heels of dog-walking San Diego State by 40 points in the opener on Monday (94-54) and No. 25 Auburn by 30 points on Tuesday (102-72), Michigan somehow saved its best for last the night before Thanksgiving. The Wolverines led by 10 points less than four minutes in and the game never got inside double digits again. They built their halftime lead out to 24 points — Gonzaga's largest deficit at the break since 2007.

In the second half, the Wolverines turned the ball over four times in the first three minutes only to get going again. Morez Johnson Jr. and Aday Mara combined for four dunks and layups while Nimari Burnett made a pair of 3s in just three minutes, ripping off a 15-2 run to go up 35 points with 12:51 to go.

The exclamation of the night came after a Johnson swat led to a Yaxel Lendeborg runout in transition, a dunk with authority and a three-point play. That's when the "Beat Ohio!" chants began, followed by yet another 15-2 run, this time in 2:49 featuring a pair of Trey McKenney 3s and yet another Lendeborg highlight, a reverse slam in transition.

Lendeborg led the way with 20 points and 11 rebounds. Burnett scored 14 points, McKenney 17, Mara 13 and Johnson 11. Elliot Cadeau set the table all night with 13 assists.

Gonzaga (7-1), which entered as KenPom's No. 1 team, was averaging 95 points a game while giving up just 62. In this one, Michigan had 53 ... at the half.

The final score marked Mark Few's largest loss in more than a quarter-century at the West Coast Conference power from Spokane, Washington.

A case for the Wolverines

Michigan (7-0) may well be the nation's No. 1 team when the next coaches poll was released Dec. 1.

"I love this team, best team I've been a part of," Lendeborg told TNT postgame. "We know if we buy in, we will be the best team in the country.

"We're capable of a national championship. ... Nobody can stop us."

Aday Mara ruled the paint against Gonzaga, making 6 of 9 shots, drawing three fouls and scoring 13 points. KIRBY LEE/IMAGN IMAGES

GONZAGA
8
15
ZAGS

Michigan isn't just a national title contender, but on the short list of favorites.

The Wolverines, who entered No. 11 in 2-point percentage (63%), continued their dominance inside. They made their first eight shots inside the arc, seven of which were dunks or layups, as well as a Mara hook from 5 feet out.

Then, Michigan got it going from long range. Burnett hit four 3-pointers, McKenney had three, and Lendeborg and Will Tschetter each made a pair. On the night, the Wolverines made 13 of 27 3-point attempts, for their third consecutive night making at least 11 shots from the long line.

It simply became a highlight reel in the second half with Lendeborg hammering down multiple slams, then throwing an alley-oop to Roddy Gayle Jr. for good measure to go up 89-43 against a team many expected to compete for a Final Four.

Gonzaga had just one answer for Michigan's quickness on the outside and length on the inside: a push shot from the middle of the lane between 8-12 feet.

Braden Huff hit a handful of them, including three in 71 seconds to get to 42-28 with 4:30 to play in the first half, but a midrange floater over a 7-foot-3 center didn't prove to be sustainable. Gonzaga, which came in as the No. 5 offense per KenPom, suffered its worst shooting night of the season in making just a third of its shots.

Perhaps the Bulldogs' legs were tired playing three straight days — Gonzaga made 3 of 22 3-pointers — but that wasn't the only reason Michigan suffocated Few's team.

Johnson, Mara and Lendeborg, the trio that make up Michigan's super-big lineup, each had a block in the first minute of the second half. Opponents still hadn't found a way to challenge the group.

Gonzaga's Graham Ike was a prime example: Averaging 17 points and nine rebounds, the 6-9 senior missed all nine of his shots en route to one point.

So ... now what?

Against San Diego State, the Wolverines led by 12 points at halftime and put it away with an 8-0 run to start the second half. The Aztecs shot only 27.4% (17 of 62) and were outscored 38-12 in the paint.

Against Auburn, the Wolverines led 15-4 after 4½ minutes and by 28 points at halftime. For the game, they outscored the Tigers 38-20 in the paint and 29-3 on fast breaks and outrebounded them 51-35. Auburn had only three assists.

The good news was Michigan could play like this. The bad news was now everybody knew it.

That didn't mean other teams would be able to compete with the Wolverines night in and night out, but they certainly wouldn't fly under the radar in any way.

The Wolverines would be held to this standard. It was impossible to play this way every single night, but Michigan was clearly capable of dominating any team in the country.

Before Michigan headed west, May said his team wouldn't be too high or too low returning from Vegas no matter what the outcome. Perhaps he didn't foresee this level of domination, and fans shouldn't expect a banner just yet.

The Wolverines were trying to lay their foundation for what could be one of their better seasons. In the process, their three dominant days in the desert would be remembered for quite some time. ■

Elliot Cadeau only scored five points but passed the ball masterfully, with 13 assists and only two turnovers. KIRBY LEE/IMAGN IMAGES

MICHIGAN
3
GONZAGA
2
ZAGS

NO. 1 WITH ASTERISK

Wolverines reach top of a poll for first time since 2013

By Tony Garcia | December 8, 2025

There's a new sheriff in town.

On the heels of its fourth consecutive victory by 30 points or more, Michigan ascended to the top of the latest USA TODAY Sports Coaches Poll.

The Wolverines (8-0, 1-0 Big Ten) had not been No. 1 in either of the two major polls since the final week of January 2013, after Michigan opened the season 16-0 and moved into February at 20-1 overall.

Michigan moved up after top-ranked Purdue was blitzed at home by Iowa State (81-58) and the Wolverines opened Big Ten play by bombing Rutgers 101-60. U-M garnered 17 of the 31 first-place votes. Next were Arizona (with 11 first-place votes), Duke (two) and Iowa State (one).

"It's funny, I've never been No. 1 or anything in my life, so I just feel like it's a great accomplishment," senior guard Roddy Gayle Jr. said. "But I feel like it's important for our guys also not to look at it as, you know, 'we're the best,' and you can't, like, slack off. ...

"We can't go in there thinking we peaked in December. We got to be able to still build all the way up to March."

The Wolverines certainly hadn't peaked in the eyes of sportswriters and sportscasters. In the Associated Press media poll, Arizona moved from No. 2 to No. 1, and U-M moved from No. 3 to No. 2. The Wildcats (also 8-0) held a 33-19 edge in first-place votes.

In the debate over the best team in America, U-M ruled in the metrics wars. The Wolverines were No. 1 on KenPom, BartTorvik and EvanMiya and in the NET rankings. Their last four victories — all over teams in Power Four leagues or with NCAA Tournament pedigree — were by a combined 151 points.

In 2013, on the 10-year anniversary of U-M's last No. 1 team, star guard Nik Stauskas sat down with the Free Press to detail the day that ranking came out. He said the players truly became celebrities on campus.

He was in a "History of Basketball" class, and his lecture stopped dead in its tracks. There was such a buzz in the air as students passed phones around showing one another the news.

The Wolverines went on to play for the national championship a little more than two months later and came up just short against Louisville 82-76 in the Trey Burke block/foul game.

Until this Monday in December, the 2013 team was the only other time U-M had been ranked No. 1 since the Fab Five days in 1992-93.

Rounding out the coaches' top 10: No. 5 Connecticut, No. 6 Purdue, No. 7 Gonzaga (which lost to U-M in Las Vegas), No. 8 Houston, No. 9 Michigan State (after a 66-60 loss to Duke) and No. 10 Brigham Young.

Three other Big Ten teams made the Top 25: No. 13 Illinois, No. 22 Nebraska (making its season debut in the poll) and No. 24 Iowa. ■

Guard L.J. Cason was a driving force off the bench as Michigan reached No. 1 until suffering a torn ACL. JUNFU HAN/DETROIT FREE PRESS

MICHIGAN
2

JANUARY 10, 2026 | ANN ARBOR, MICHIGAN
WISCONSIN 91, NO. 1 MICHIGAN 88

AT A LOSS

Wolverines aren't invincible — as they learn the hard way

By Tony Garcia

Michigan's first loss of the season — a 91-88 thriller against Wisconsin — was likely a surprise for most fans.

But players and coaches saw the seeds planted for that result over the past two weeks —with four consecutive games without the Wolverines feeling they had played up to their standard.

"The right team won," coach Dusty May said after a loss certain to drop his team from the top of the coaches poll.

Michigan (14-1, 4-1 Big Ten) led by 14 points with 7:38 left in the first half but let Wisconsin (11-5, 3-2) back into the game with a 20-7 run going into halftime. The run included three 3-pointers, part of the Badgers' season-high 15 3s.

"Give Wisconsin credit," May said. "They came in here, took a punch early, they responded and went in at halftime with positive momentum. They came out in the second half and knocked us on our heels a little bit.

"They made plays. Our plan, our coaching, our playing wasn't up to our standard."

It was similar to U-M's game earlier in the week, when the Wolverines allowed Penn State to go on a 12-0 second-half run before escaping with a 74-72 victory in Happy Valley.

At Crisler Center, however, the bill came due for the Wolverines by not going hard in practice — where U-M had done the work behind its 14-0 start to the season.

"To be honest, the only thing I'm disappointed in is when we started playing, competing at a high level, it looked different," May said. "We can't be a team, with what we're playing for, that has two different levels of intensity."

'They exposed some things'

One of Michigan's few flaws during the season had been dealing with stretch bigs. That was especially apparent after Wisconsin freshman Aleksas Bieliauskas drilled five 3-pointers, including four in less than three minutes of the second half.

Aday Mara was a fantastic rim protector, but he's not built to move out to the arc. When bigs who can shoot are able to pull him away from the basket, it's a problem.

"We changed our coverages, changed our personnel; we didn't do a good enough job," May said. "We worked three days on that. ... We knew it was coming, you know it's coming. ... When they make the first couple, there's such an overreaction.

"They exposed some things with our plan and our team that we thought were going to be issues this year."

The Wolverines began sticking with the Badgers harder on the perimeter, fighting over screens instead of going under them. The change slowed Wisconsin's 3-point shooting — the Badgers closed the game 3-for-10 beyond the arc after making 12 of their first 23 — but it also allowed more dribble-drive penetration, mostly by Nick Boyd.

Yaxel Lendeborg and Aday Mara were bummed as Wisconsin handed Michigan its first loss. JUNFU HAN/DETROIT FREE PRESS

B1G
MICHIGAN
23
B1G
MICHIGAN
15

He scored 22 points against U-M and May, his coach at Florida Atlantic. That was second only to Wisconsin's John Blackwell, who had 26 points — the third double-digit scoring game in four tries by the Birmingham Brother Rice alum against the school that passed on him.

"They did a good job of exploiting the mismatches and finding a way to get open," said Nimari Burnett, who scored 10 points. "We can take this lesson and apply it to other games."

'Got to find some solutions'

Michigan was solid on offense, at least, topping 80 points for the 13th time in 15 games.

Elliot Cadeau — who sat much of the first half in foul trouble — frequently thrived in one-on-one situations en route to 19 points, his second-best total this season. Morez Johnson Jr. missed just one of his seven shots and finished with 18 points.

But for the fourth game in a row, U-M shot under 33% on 3s, going 8-for-25 (32%).

"We've got to find some solutions to get better shots," May said.

The game was knotted at 81 with 4:53 to play. Roddy Gayle Jr. put U-M ahead 84-83 with a corner 3, but it would be the Wolverines' next-to-last basket. Blackwell answered with a driving layup. U-M couldn't sink anything but stayed close because Blackwell and Braeden Carrington missed the front end of one-and-ones.

A slashing bucket by Gayle make it 88-86 with 1:11 to play. After Mara blocked a shot and Andrew Rohde missed, Mara appeared to have a put-back slam off a Gayle missed layup with 35.2 seconds left. But Mara was called for offensive goaltending — the ball just barely hanging on the cylinder. The call went to review and stood.

Instead of a tied game, Carrington made two free throws for a 90-86 lead. Burnett missed two 3-pointers in the ensuing possession, but Yaxel Lendeborg made two free throws to make it 90-88 with 15 seconds left.

U-M got its break when Carrington split two free throws and got the ball with nine seconds left. But Gayle missed a leaning 3-pointer in the final seconds.

The Wolverines missed eight of their final nine shots.

'Processes have to improve'

Shooting comes and goes, as May and Co. have tried to point out. Effort should not, though.

But Wisconsin got more second-chance points (15-8) and was virtually even in rebounding.

Michigan won its first 14 games in large part because of superior talent. While that's a prerequisite for a deep March run, the grind behind the scenes was every bit as important.

Of Michigan's three days of prep from Tuesday to Saturday, Cadeau and May said, only one was acceptable.

"Our processes have to improve, our practice habits, our day-to-day habits have to be at a championship level," May said. "Or we're simply going to rely on the other team not playing up to their standard or our talent. That's not a real healthy way to get through the Big Ten season."

The Penn State victory offered solace that when the going got tough, the Wolverines would find a way. Faltering against Wisconsin wiped away that illusion.

Michigan's goals — a Big Ten title, a March Madness run — were all still attainable. But only if the Wolverines felt this sting and played with the same desire opponents were bringing against them, night in and night out.

Even in practice.

"It's like a smack in our face," Burnett said. "No team is going to go undefeated — obviously, we hoped to do it — but like I said, just need to learn from it." ■

Nimari Burnett (4) and Roddy Gayle Jr. endured a rough afternoon against the Badgers. JUNFU HAN/DETROIT FREE PRESS

32
4
2
For fun.

JANUARY 23, 2026 | ANN ARBOR, MICHIGAN

NO. 2 MICHIGAN 74, OHIO STATE 62

BURKE'S BOAST

His number in the rafters, he wants a 2026 banner to follow

By Tony Garcia

Arguably the best point guard to wear a Michigan jersey was on hand for the latest stellar performance from Dusty May's group.

Trey Burke's No. 3 jersey rose to the Crisler Center rafters during halftime of U-M's 74-62 victory over Ohio State during a ceremony in which he thanked the crowd for turning a Columbus boy into an Ann Arbor man. After the contest, he took over the mic and shared the same message he just had told players on the court with the fans who stayed.

"National championship or bust," he said. "This group can do that."

Earlier this Friday night, arguably the greatest Michigan basketball coach of all-time —certainly the winningest — in John Beilein, detailed what he felt was the common thread of the two teams he led in Ann Arbor to national title games.

Elite guard play.

This season's iteration of the Wolverines had been defined by its bigs, and they starred against the Buckeyes. Yaxel Lendeborg, in his best game in weeks, put up 18 points and nine rebounds. Morez Johnson Jr. delivered one of the quieter 12-point, seven-rebound performances — though his alley-oop slam that gave Michigan a 52-50 lead it wouldn't relinquish was mighty loud on its own. Aday Mara was an eraser at the rim and made timely plays — and, for once, free throws — as he finished with 11 points, six boards, four blocks and two steals.

But when it was winning time, as the second half reached its key moment, it was a pair of guards who rose above for Michigan.

Elliott Cadeau and Trey McKenney combined to score or assist on 11 points during a 19-5 run that turned a one-point contest into a 15-point lead in just 4:35 of court time. Neither guard's stat line was flashy in the end: McKenney scored 12 points and Cadeau had six points and eight assists.

But each played their best in the second half during winning time.

"I think our guard play has to be exceptional; (Beilein) is right," May said. "If Elliot and L.J. (Cason) and Trey and Roddy (Gayle Jr.) and Nimari (Burnett) don't play well, we're not going to be a national title contender."

'He's such a pest'

Cadeau sputtered in the first half — a pair of early fouls, three assists and two turnovers — as Michigan had a tough time with its zone offense, for a 33-30 lead at the break. McKenney had three points and three rebounds.

But when Michigan trailed 40-34 — its largest deficit against Ohio State (13-6, 5-4 Big Ten) — they

Trey Burke addressed fans as his No. 3 jersey was raised to the rafters at Crisler Center. JUNFU HAN/DETROIT FREE PRESS

MICHIGAN
M
BURKE
3

showed up. McKenney made two free throws and Cadeau forced a turnover at midcourt (as part of a full-court press) and threw a feed to Lendeborg to knot the game at 40.

McKenney capped off an 11-0 spurt with a layup through contact for a three-point play, sending the sellout crowd to its feet. After OSU retook the lead, Gayle grabbed an offensive rebound for a putback, and Cason slashed through the paint for a left-handed finger roll.

After OSU knotted it again at 50, Cadeau threw a lob to Johnson for a slam. Then, the current No. 3's 3-pointer, for U-M's next bucket, sent another jolt through the crowd — almost as large as the one after his 3 from the same spot just more than a minute later.

It came as little surprise to Lendeborg, who said Cadeau had been "carrying" the Wolverines.

May concurred.

"It just felt like that allowed us to continue the momentum that we were building," May said. "We trust him as a shooter, trust him as a floor general, and then defensively, he's such a pest. I mean, he plays with discipline. He's as impactful as any guard in our conference."

History in the making?

This was the second time in four seasons Burke returned to Crisler Center.

In February 2023, he came back, with Beilein and numerous other players, to celebrate the 10th anniversary of Michigan's 2013 national runner-up squad.

This U-M team could return a decade from now for a similar celebration or perhaps more. The second-ranked Wolverines (18-1, 8-1) are No. 1 in most advanced metrics and just a half-game out of the Big Ten lead. The team ahead of them, unbeaten No. 7 Nebraska, was set to come to Ann Arbor next week.

But ahead of that, the Wolverines heard Burke's message and knew a special season was brewing.

"I mean, that's definitely the motto for us," McKenney said. "That's what we came in this summer thinking and working towards every day. So, I mean I would definitely agree."

May was asked how much he could appreciate a season like this happening in the moment. He shied away from the question before detailing what awaited in what he called a "monster" week — following Nebraska a road clash with two-loss and 10th-ranked Michigan State.

"I think as a coach," he said, "you savor those things later."

Later will come all too soon, especially if the Wolverines falter in March Madness as many great teams have. Nothing is destined. It will take the same work, if not more, than it had through these 19 games.

Burke didn't win it all, though he was as close as it got without having done so. Same with Beilein, twice over.

Burke and Beilein said this team had the goods. That certainly was true if the guards went from good to great.

"I don't take those words lightly," Lendeborg said. "I want to fulfill what (Burke) said." ■

Morez Johnson Jr. stymied Ohio State's Christoph Tilly during the second half of Michigan's victory. JUNFU HAN/DETROIT FREE PRESS

MICHIGAN
21
TILLY
13
OHIO
21
STATE

JANUARY 27, 2026 | ANN ARBOR, MICHIGAN

NO. 2 MICHIGAN 75, NO. 5 NEBRASKA 72

BEATING AN UNBEATEN

Displaying 'winning DNA,' Wolverines move into tie for first

By Tony Garcia

Outside of basketball, Dusty May is generally not an abstract thinker.

In the sport he coaches? Sure. On the hardwood, he plays to the analytics and visualizes how a roster comes together even before it shares a court.

Otherwise? May is more grounded in the play in any given 40 minutes, on approximately 75 possessions a night.

But when it came to Michigan's ability to get dirty on an off night to knock off previously undefeated Nebraska 75-72 and grab a share of first place in the Big Ten?

That brought out the one philosophy he does subscribe to.

"I do believe in winning DNA," May said after No. 2 Michigan (19-1, 9-1 Big Ten) tied its best 20-game start ever. "I believe in the look that you just, you feel like you're going to find a way — no matter how it's going, what's happened up to this point, how it's going for me individually.

"The shared belief of the guys in the circle with you that they prepared for this. ... I believe you make your own luck."

Michigan certainly made its own mess. Despite the Cornhuskers (20-1, 9-1) being down a pair of starters who are two of their top three scorers, U-M's defense allowed 50 points in the first half, on 59.4% shooting — their second-worst mark in a half — first or second. The offense? It shot 23.1% on 3-pointers for the game and had 18 turnovers, including six in a six-minute span early in the second half.

But the Wolverines also were clutch, making 14 of 17 free throws in the second half. They switched their ball screen defense and forced more contested looks beyond the arc —Nebraska hit just one of 13 3s after the break. And, eventually, Michigan made the plays it needed to, going on a 10-2 run over the final 5:51 en route to its final lead with 67 seconds left — U-M's first lead since 85 seconds in — to eke out a victory when little else went right.

Does Michigan need to play cleaner? *Of course.*

May called fixing U-M's turnover woes his "top priority."

Does it need to shoot better? *Of course.*

That should come if Michigan continues to generate open looks.

But what happened at a rambunctious Crisler Center was no fluke: It was a team leaning into its crunch-time principles.

"Sticking together," said forward Morez Johnson Jr., who led the team with 17 points and 12 rebounds. "Not pulling away from each other. Staying as one, talking to each other, being more physical."

Trey McKenney and the Wolverines topped the Nebraska Cornhuskers with a thrilling comeback. JUNFU HAN/DETROIT FREE PRESS

HIGAN
1
N
DFORT

Freshman growth apparent

Michigan wouldn't have won without freshman and McDonald's All-American Trey McKenney, who had 11 points in 22 minutes — his second-best outing in a competitive Big Ten game.

The first six of those points came on two first-half 3s to keep U-M's deficit reasonable.

"He's not the same player as he was in November," Johnson said. "He's very important for us. When he comes off the bench, he gives us that boost of energy every time he's on the floor. We know what we're going to get out of Trey every night."

Michigan trailed by seven with less than eight minutes to play when McKenney drew a foul on a 3-point attempt. He then calmly and confidently buried all three free throws — "the biggest points of the game," May called them.

But his two biggest points came with 67 seconds left. With the Cornhuskers on the run, McKenney swiped the ball on a back-poke to start U-M's half-court offense. In that, Yaxel Lendeborg drove to the paint and then whipped an overhand pass, where McKenney was waiting in the weak-side corner.

He pump-faked, jabbed right and then drove the baseline before meeting Sam Hoiberg's chest and finishing a floating layup over him for a 74-72 lead.

"The baseline was kind of open because they were, you know, forcing us to the baseline, they wouldn't give us middle drives," McKenney said. "Had to take advantage of that."

Just enough plays

It wasn't just McKenney, of course.

Will Tschetter had U-M's only 3-pointer of the second half, plus two free throws and a basket underneath. Lendeborg missed all his 3s, but made all four free throws. Johnson made 6 of 7 free throws, while Michigan scored 12 of its 16 points from the stripe in the final 9:55.

"We stepped up and we made big free throws," May said. "Especially at winning time. ... When you're down four and five and three, like we were, those are the hardest ones to make, because they're all so pressure-filled."

Michigan was in that spot, however, because of its mistakes. Elliott Cadeau had a season-high eight turnovers. Some of them, May could live with. But overall, that many mistakes often won't cut it.

"We continue to turn the ball over like we have last couple games. ... We're gonna be playing from behind a lot," May said. "I don't think we did a lot of things well, but just our sheer determination to win the last four or five minutes was impressive."

Michigan has another game requiring the same intensity — if not more — in three days at East Lansing. No. 8 Michigan State had its struggles in beating Rutgers in overtime on Tuesday.

But each of U-M's victories had built toward the rivalry, including knocking off the Big Ten's final undefeated team.

"These games are awesome," May said. "Is it perfect? No, but college basketball is in a pretty good place. I know you're not gonna hear that very often, but if you just look at that two hours, man, that's a heck of a college basketball game.

"Hats off to Nebraska. They're gonna win a lot of games. They're top 5 in the country for a reason, and it's on to the next. You gotta get ready for Sparty." ■

Nebraska's defense held Yaxel Lendeborg to 10 points on 3-for-10 shooting, 0-for-6 from long distance. JUNFU HAN/DETROIT FREE PRESS

Nebraska
31
23
LAWRENCE
10
Nebraska
9
WHY SO SERIOUS

JANUARY 30, 2026 | EAST LANSING, MICHIGAN

NO. 2 MICHIGAN 83, NO. 8 MICHIGAN STATE 71

BRESLIN BUSTERS

For first time since 2018, Wolverines triumph in East Lansing

By Carlos Monarrez

Anyone who expected a heavyweight bout between Michigan and Michigan State got something even more physical.

They got an all-out street fight with bodies littering every corner of the floor at Breslin Center on a Friday night.

OK, so that's also most Big Ten games in East Lansing.

But then there was this. Wolverine against Spartan. *Hate against hate.* Two top-10 teams battling for the conference lead and a whole lot more. Namely, *respect.*

Especially on Michigan's side, which the Wolverines, ranked No. 2 in this week's USA TODAY Sports Coaches Poll, deservedly got with an 83-71 victory.

It was a victory that looked like it might be an early round knockout for Michigan when it took advantage of MSU's cold shooting and took a 42-26 lead into halftime.

The eighth-ranked Spartans came out of the break looking like expert counterpunchers, opening the second half with a 15-4 run. With 7:27 left, MSU took its first lead, 57-55, after Jeremy Fears Jr. scored on a layup off a turnover.

"So, that one obviously didn't feel good," said forward Yaxel Lendeborg, who led U-M with 26 points and 12 rebounds. "But we all knew how tough it was going to be when they came back, because they weren't just going to lay down for us.

"So, they gave us that haymaker, you know? We kept jabbing back until we got back on our feet and got back there constantly. So, it was a good recovery by us."

Indeed, the Wolverines didn't spend much time on the canvas. Thanks to U-M's composure, consistent rebounding and steady work in the paint, MSU's lead was short-lived — all of 24 seconds.

"Yeah, man," Lendeborg said, "like usually, you know, we all get like fidgety and jittery, you know? Just start getting worried, you know? Nobody had that look in their eye this time. You know, we all just huddled up a little closer. You know, nobody was screaming at each other. We all stay composed. And again, it goes back to maturity. You know, we just did our best to stay mature."

Bigger than life or death?

The Wolverines had lost seven straight at Breslin, where they hadn't tasted victory since Jan. 13, 2018. That's 2,939 days. It was a stretch so long that, when U-M last won in East Lansing, Dusty May hadn't even gotten his first job as a head coach.

En route to 12 points, Morez Johnson Jr. made a statement against MSU's Carson Cooper. JUNFU HAN/DETROIT FREE PRESS

COOPER
15

A year ago, May was on his second head coaching job and his first season at Michigan when he was baptized by fire in the Red Cedar River. He got his second taste of this rivalry during Logo-gate on MSU's senior day in March. He said he learned that the Wolverines had placed too much emphasis on the game itself and their opponent.

This year, he decided to borrow a page from the Indiana Hoosiers, the newly crowned College Football Playoff champions from his home state, whose coach, Curt Cignetti, downplayed a crucial meeting this season at Penn State by saying that year's team had never played in State College.

"But this team that we have in our locker room," he said, "they were 0-0. And so, we're not talking about what the past teams have done."

There was just one problem with May's plan: His players weren't exactly buying it.

Because they heard it everywhere around Ann Arbor from their fellow students. Basketball isn't football, but the basketball rivalry with MSU is the closest thing the Wolverines have to the animosity they feel toward Ohio State in football.

"Absolutely, man," Lendeborg said. "So many DM's I was getting from Michigan fans, begging us to win this game, you know?

"And it's like you would think they're about to lose their life if we lose, you know? So, it's like I don't want to let those guys down."

May also admitted what the game meant to the Michigan faithful.

"Obviously, this is important for our fans," he said. "But for us, this was more about winning a Big Ten game on the road and staying in a hunt, because we've got a very challenging schedule coming up."

Dogfight down the stretch

The victory vaulted U-M (20-1) to the top of the conference standings with a 10-1 record and capped an impressive week that included a 75-72 triumph over previously undefeated Nebraska. The Spartans fell to 19-3 and 9-2.

The Wolverines get to rest until their tilt against Penn State back in Ann Arbor.

But that game was nearly a week away. As he stood deep inside Breslin, Lendeborg was just thinking about the bus ride home and the reception that awaited his team.

"Oh, my gosh, man, we're all excited to go home, you know?" he said. "Just see all the Michigan fans, talk to whoever we can and just celebrate this win." ■

With hair flying and Spartans flailing, Elliot Cadeau hunted for a route to the basket at Breslin Center. JUNFU HAN/DETROIT FREE PRESS

BIG

THE BIG THREE

How Michigan built the nation's biggest and best frontcourt

By Tony Garcia | February 15, 2026

Their paths to Ann Arbor could hardly be more different.

For one, it was Spain to California to Michigan.

Another left Puerto Rico for New Jersey, with stops in Arizona and Alabama, then zoomed north.

And then there's the Midwesterner, heading south in Illinois, from Riverdale to Champaign, before arriving in the Great Lakes State.

And yet, despite those disparate distances covered, they wound up in one place, with one goal, with one team: the Michigan Wolverines.

Aday Mara, Yaxel Lendeborg and Morez Johnson Jr. — the "Big Three" for coach Dusty May — are all on their second stop in Division I basketball, each poised to spend next season in the NBA as first-round picks. But first, each is looking to make history with the Wolverines.

At 24-1 overall and 14-1 in the Big Ten, Michigan is off to its best start in history and now prepares for a regular-season finish that features four of the nation's top 12 teams in 20 days.

But before looking ahead — to No. 12 Purdue on Tuesday, No. 6 Duke on Saturday, No. 7 Illinois on Feb. 28 and, finally, No. 10 Michigan State on March 8 — it's worth a moment to look back at how they all arrived in Ann Arbor and how they learned to thrive together.

"I think they trusted us," May told the Free Press in January. "The people that advised them said they could trust us."

In May's first year, the Wolverines had made a surprising surge from the bottom of the Big Ten to a Sweet 16 appearance, thanks to a pair of 7-foot transfers, Vlad Goldin (from FAU) and Danny Wolf (from Yale). Could they go even farther with *three* bigs?

"I think the Danny and Vlad experiment gave us a little bit of credibility that we will figure it out when everyone else was saying that we couldn't," May said. "But as far as having to sell them on it? No, we just presented what our vision was and hoped they'd buy into it."

They're coming together

That they did.

Johnson was first, committing to the Wolverines on April 1, 2025, after one season at Illinois. Less than two weeks later, Mara jumped from UCLA after two seasons. Lendeborg took a little longer to decide his destination after two seasons at Alabama-Birmingham; the No. 1 prospect in the transfer portal debated between Ann Arbor and the NBA draft.

That was fine with May and the Wolverines; U-M's staff met with Lendeborg sporadically (including at the NBA scouting combine) and arranged visits for him to see the facilities, giving him a vision of how

Michigan big men and potential first-round draft picks (from the left) Aday Mara, Yaxel Lendeborg and Morez Johnson Jr. transferred to Ann Abor for the 2025-26 season and formed arguably the country's top frontcourt. JUNFU HAN/DETROIT FREE PRESS

MARA
15
MICHIGAN
23
21

he would fit with the other bigs.

Lendeborg liked U-M's approach — no forced decisions or hard deadlines. And so, nearly 50 days after Johnson and Mara jumped, Lendeborg withdrew from the NBA draft and committed to Michigan.

May celebrated with staff, then quickly made a phone call.

"I didn't know what to expect at first — when I first heard ... I was just in shock and Dusty called me," Johnson said. "He was telling me how it's going to work, I'm like,"OK, OK.' I just had trust in it, believed what he was saying and hoped he would keep his word.

"That's what he did."

They're going to work

Johnson arrived in Ann Arbor about a week after committing. Soon after that, he was a fixture in the gym, with a work ethic U-M general manager Kyle Church described as "maniacal" a mere month later.

But Johnson didn't stay in Ann Arbor for long. By the time Lendeborg and Mara arrived, Johnson was in Switzerland with the USA U-19 team that won gold. He returned later in the summer, but by then, he and Mara were dealing with lingering injuries — and seeing all three on the court was a rarity.

Mara, meanwhile, was simply happy Johnson was in the fold.

"I actually thought you were going to UCLA," Mara told Johnson months later, at a sit-down interview with the Free Press.

Johnson made a face and simply said, "Nah."

But by fall, all three were running practices together and figuring out how to play in their new roles. Lendeborg was used to being the focal point of an offense in the paint. Johnson had been a rim runner for the Illini. Mara, meanwhile, was learning to share space down low with others for the first time.

Of the three, Lendeborg had the most adapting to do.

"At first it was kind of an adjustment, because I know I really had to become a shooter in order to make sure we can all stay on the floor together," Lendeborg said. "I had high hopes for how it was gonna go, and it's been going better than I thought."

At first, though? U-M lost its exhibition opener to Cincinnati, despite 31 points and 12 rebounds from Lendeborg. The regular season barely started better: Unbeaten, but with a clunky offense featuring less than a point per possession with the trio on the court.

Then, it all clicked in the desert.

"In Vegas, for sure," Lendeborg said. "I feel like that's when my 3-point shot started to come along, and I started feeling way more confident in myself. That really helped the spacing a lot more because I didn't have to rely on being in the paint."

In U-M's opener in the Players Era Festival in Las Vegas during Thanksgiving week, the three combined for 35 points and 20 boards against San Diego State. The next night, against Auburn, it was 37 points and 18 boards. They closed out the tourney with a 40-point rout of No. 7 Gonzaga with 44 points and 22 boards, despite only Lendeborg playing for more than 23 minutes.

'He could be anywhere'

Three frontcourt stars, all of whom arrived as developed players — it didn't take long for accusations of "mercenaries" to land on the Michigan trio.

Not from May, however. He reiterated in February the sacrifice needed to lift the Wolverines to their lofty perch in the Big Ten. It started with Lendeborg, averaging 14.3 points and 7.7 boards a game — respectable numbers, but not what might have

Noted for their unselfishness, Yaxel Lendeborg (left) and Morez Johnson Jr. shared a high-five. JUNFU HAN/DETROIT FREE PRESS

B1G
MICHIGAN
21

been expected from a forward projected as a late first-round NBA selection last summer and definitely not from a potential lottery pick in 2026.

"(Yaxel) set the tone," Johnson said. "Like, if he's willing to sacrifice things for the team, everyone should be able to sacrifice things for the team. Lord knows he could be anywhere, somewhere else in the country, just getting shots up, trying to get his numbers."

Lendeborg, who spent his first three seasons in juco at Arizona Western, had been willing to give up touches to make sure his teammates were involved.

"He doesn't act like a mercenary every day," May said. "He's completely engrossed and embedded in our program, our culture and winning for others. He's unique. He's special. ... We wouldn't be where we are if it wasn't for his unselfishness and his humility as a guy that was ranked as the No. 1" player in the portal.

Together, the trio formed what was widely regarded as the best frontcourt in the nation. Mara was top-10 in the nation in block rate. Lendeborg (25) and Johnson (27) were among the nation's best in offensive rating per KenPom. They all averaged 10-15 points with at least seven rebounds and more than one block a game.

Johnson said the three felt like they had an advantage whenever they stepped on the court. Mara concurred. Lendeborg went a step further.

"I already said this like three times, but I don't think there's a frontcourt that's better than ours," he said. "I'll go to war with these guys every day about it.

'A soft teddy bear'

As they meshed on the court, they melded off it, as well.

Mara was the one who cooked "on and off the court," Johnson said. Mara said Lendeborg's most surprising trait was his humility: "Maybe (outsiders would) think that he's another way, but he's super humble."

Johnson, however — according to Lendeborg, at least — was the one whose demeanor changed most when he was not playing.

"Morez is a super-tough guy on the court man, but off the court, he" really just a soft teddy bear," Lendeborg said as all three laughed. "When you talk to him a little bit, he's really just a sweetie."

When asked about the others' best trait, the answers were unanimous. For Johnson, it's his elite rebounding instincts. For Mara, it's his incredible length and shot-blocking skills. Lendeborg? He can "do it all," Mara said.

One of those skills was passing, a skill Mara exceled at considering his 7-foot-3 stature.

"(Their passing) opens up everything," Johnson said. "Having players who will pass, you know, that helps because you can't really go double Aday or Yax or me, because we all capable passers."

Johnson liked to consider himself a passer, too, even if the others disagreed.

As they chatted in mid-January, Mara grinned as a wide-eyed Lendeborg asked Johnson, "How many assists you got this year?"

Johnson said 25 as Lendeborg whipped out his phone to pull up the numbers.

During the web search, Johnson backtracked slightly: "It's got to be at least 20."

The answer: 18.

"They haven't added last game yet," Johnson said.

"Yes, they have," Lendeborg said with a chuckle, showing him the phone.

One eye on the future

March Madness remained more than a month away, but everything was lining up for the Wolverines, who had a two-game lead in the Big Ten race, a likely No. 1 ranking in the next poll and a projected 1-seed in the NCAA Tournament come next month.

Much of that success had been fueled by the frontcourt, which spent the past four months proving the naysayers wrong.

"When one of them committed and then the next one committed, they were both told by everyone that

Aday Mara joined Michigan after two seasons at UCLA and emerged as one of the nation's top shot blockers. JUNFU HAN/DETROIT FREE PRESS

they couldn't work," May said. "'*Why would you do that? You're not going to play.*' ... When we got all three of them, then it became overload. ... All the original schools recruiting them all circled back to that: '*You can't play together.*'"

As it turned out, they could.

Johnson was shooting 69.4% on 2-pointers, a mark that would be No. 2 in U-M history. Lendeborg was a member of most All-Big Ten first-team projections. Mara was averaging career highs in points, rebounds, blocks and minutes.

The Wolverines' historic success hadn't prevented anybody from looking forward, however.

"In a perfect world, these three guys are playing in the Association as first-round picks next year," May said. "They're incredibly important to us, too and we have one eye pointed towards their future and their developments. Even when we're working extra on things they're not doing now in games, it's to help them down the line."

Those days would come soon enough.

In the meantime, the trio had some business to finish in their shared hometown. ■

CONSENSUS NO. 1

A month later, Wolverines sit atop the coaches and media polls

By Tony Garcia | February 16, 2026

There's a new No. 1 team in the nation. And it's an old No. 1 team.

Plus, this time, it was a consensus No. 1 team.

Michigan moved up one spot to once again headline the USA TODAY Sports Coaches Poll. The Wolverines were last atop the poll in its Jan. 5 iteration — five days before their loss to Wisconsin, still their only defeat.

Michigan also moved up one spot to lead the Associated Press media poll. During their five weeks atop the coaches poll in December and early January, the Wolverines were stuck at No. 2 behind Arizona in the media poll.

Since losing to the Badgers, Michigan ripped off 10 straight victories, nine by double digits. U-M received all 31 first-place votes from the coaches and 60 of 61 first-place votes from sportswriters and sportscasters.

The Wolverines, though, were in dire straits on Feb. 11 against Northwestern. Mired in an offensive funk, they trailed the Wildcats by 16 points (58-42) with 14:22 left to play. L.J. Carson emerged as the unlikely hero, replacing Elliot Cadeau with 15:15 left and playing the point the rest of the game. He hit 3 of 4 shots and made 6 of 6 free throws for 13 second-half points with three assists and only one turnover. U-M rode a 21-7 run to an 87-75 victory.

Three days later, U-M blitzed UCLA 86-56 as Aday Mara, only needed for 23 minutes, posted nine points, eight rebounds, three blocks and three assists against his old team.

Michigan could move up because Arizona lost for the first time, dropping back-to-back Big 12 games — 82-78 at No. 9 Kansas and 78-75 in overtime against No. 16 Texas Tech. The Wolverines were the only one-loss team left among the Power Five conferences.

"Our goal is not being No. 1 in the country," Mara said. "Our goal is to win everything."

Nine of the top 10 teams were identical in the two polls: 1, Michigan (24-1). 2, Houston (23-2). 3, Duke (23-2). 4, Arizona (23-2). 5, Connecticut (24-2). 6, Iowa State (22-3). 7, Purdue (21-4). 8, DISAGREEMENT. 9, Nebraska (22-3). 10, Illinois (21-5). At No. 9, the coaches chose Kansas (19-6) while the media went with Gonzaga (25-2).

Michigan's second reign at the top would be in jeopardy immediately: The next day, U-M would play at Purdue. Come Saturday, they would play Duke at Washington.

Michigan had been ranked No. 1 for 38 games in its 108-year history.

Feb. 16 marked the latest in a season Michigan had No. 1 since it was No. 1 in the AP poll on March 7, 1977, the final poll before the NCAA Tournament. Soon after, the Wolverines were upset by Charlotte in the Elite Eight.

Prior to that, Michigan hadn't been ranked No. 1 in February or later since 1965. That year Cazzie Russell led the Wolverines to the national championship game, which U-M lost to UCLA after holding onto the nation's top spot for more than three months. ■

A spark plug off the bench who averaged 8.4 points, L.J. Carson bamboozled the Buckeyes. JUNFU HAN/DETROIT FREE PRESS

MICHIGAN
2
OHIO
2
STATE
31
1ST HALF
41.3
30

FEBRUARY 21, 2026 | WASHINGTON, D.C.
NO. 3 DUKE 68, NO. 1 MICHIGAN 63

BEDEVILED!

Duke delivers U-M humbling lessons, but not devastating ones

By Tony Garcia

There's never a great time to learn a tough lesson, but a nonconference game, with no bearing on the Big Ten standings, at a neutral site, might be the best one.

Top-ranked Michigan lost to No. 3 Duke 68-63 at Capital One Arena in a nationally televised Saturday night showdown that played much closer than even a five-point spread.

As coach Dusty May said after the fact, "Am I glad we lost? No."

And yet, it didn't damage the Wolverines' chances of a Big Ten championship. It didn't knock U-M off the 1-seed line. Most importantly, it gave the Wolverines a legitimate Final Four-level test, facing a fellow likely 1-seed in a March Madness-type environment. That the Wolverines lost showed them what must be done against other top teams.

"We know more about our team now; we'll be better because of this game," May said. "We didn't rebound the way we needed to, and we made some timely errors. ... But, proud of our guys: We fought, competed, overcame adversity and stayed together.

"There are several learning lessons we'll have from this film."

The struggles were easy to point out: Michigan scored its fewest points this season. It lost on the glass (41-28) by its largest margin. It was outscored in the paint (34-24) in ways that hadn't happened. On top of all that, the Wolverines' 24% success rate on 3-pointers was their worst in nearly a month.

U-M also was hamstrung by Aday Mara playing just six minutes in the first half due to three quick fouls. Considering all of that, it's almost impressive that Michigan only lost by five.

Now, let's be clear: Michigan was beyond looking for moral victories.

But to know that Elliot Cadeau, Nimari Burnett and Trey McKenney made just two of a combined 17 shots and it was still a one-possession game in the final minute. It's an argument that the Wolverines were right where they wanted to be, as long as the execution was there.

Duke played a role in U-M's struggles, too; the second-largest team in America made the Wolverines fight for points in the spaces they normally dominated.

"Defensively, (Duke is) a lot better than everybody else in the Big Ten in my opinion," said Yaxel Lendeborg, who led U-M with 21 points despite just five in the second half. "They have a lot of athletes."

Michigan missed nine shots in a row over a 6:09 stretch midway through the second half. It still never trailed by more than eight points, and the Wolverines rallied quickly with seven straight points in less than two minutes to pull within one with 3:49 to play.

But from there, U-M gave up a lob for a slam, then conceded a Cameron Boozer 3-pointer from the left wing for a two-possession deficit the Wolverines wound up unable to overcome. Boozer was the best player on the court, too, as he finished with 18 points,

A spectacular freshman, Cameron Boozer had 18 points, 10 rebounds and seven assists against Michigan. BOB DONNAN/IMAGN IMAGES

10 boards and seven assists despite sitting for four minutes in the second half with foul trouble.

Michigan's front line had been able to stymie virtually every opponent in the paint, but Boozer had his way, particularly on the glass, grabbing four of Duke's 13 offensive boards, which led to 18 second-chance points.

"Michigan is a physical team," Boozer said. "If you don't match that physicality and take it up a notch, it's going to hurt you."

That's what was most surprising about this result: *How* it happened.

Duke got fully half of its points (34) in the paint. U-M tried Lendeborg and Morez Johnson Jr. (who had 13 points and six boards) on Boozer, but he forced U-M's bigs into foul trouble and went 5-for-8 on 2s against one of the nation's top three teams in stopping those shots.

"I would say it was shocking," Lendeborg said. "There were times we were talking to each other on the court like, 'We can't allow any more 2s,' and that's the first time I've ever heard anybody in our circle (have) to say that. It was kind of frustrating because we thought we were playing pretty good defense. ... We got a lot to fix." ■

FEBRUARY 27, 2026 | CHAMPAIGN, ILLINOIS

NO. 3 MICHIGAN 84, NO. 11 ILLINOIS 70

THE B1G'S BEST

Despite heckling, Johnson clinches Big Ten title with double-double

By USA TODAY Network

On the night that Michigan clinched its 10th Big Ten championship and first since 2021, the Wolverines stood up for Morez Johnson Jr. as Illinois' Orange Krush mercilessly heckled him, ended a nine-game losing streak to the Illini, celebrated with a trophy in their locker room and worried about a knee injury suffered by L.J. Cason.

A top-10 showdown (according to the Associated Press poll) and the return of Johnson to Champaign (11 months after transferring to Ann Arbor) on a Friday night electrified the crowd at the State Farm Center. The student section sported signs of Johnson in clown makeup and a traitor jersey and booed and cursed at him starting with pregame warmups. Ten students behind the Illini bench painted "MIRK > MOREZ" on their chests to assert their preference for freshman David Mirkovic. Fans booed each time Johnson touched the ball.

Michigan had his back from start to finish. Yaxel Lendeborg wore Johnson's No. 21 jersey during warmups. Johnson led the team onto the court. In closing seconds of an 84-70 victory, Michigan put the ball in Johnson's hands to dribble out the clock.

In between, Michigan's big men rocked the Illini, none more so than Johnson. He had 13 first-half points on his way to double-double of 19 points and 11 rebounds. He went 6 of 10 from the field and 6 of 8 from the line.

"Morez had a night," Illini coach Brad Underwood said. "He's a next-level guy, and he showed that."

"Morez, from the jump ball, was a force," U-M coach Dusty May said. "I thought his defense was equally as impressive as his offense, being able to guard bigs, guard smalls. He's such a competitor. His day-to-day, his minute-by-minute is as impressive as any player I've ever been around."

Aday Mara made 11 of 12 shots — 8-for-9 from the field, 3-for-3 from the line — en route to 19 points. Lendeborg filled the stat sheet with 16 points, seven rebounds, four assists, two blocks and two steals while playing 38:34.

Michigan (27-2, 17-1 Big Ten) led by seven points at the half and then stretched it to 10 twice but couldn't put away the Illini (22-7, 13-5). Finally, a 13-2 run midway through the half established a 14-point lead. Mara contributed seven straight points in 66 seconds during the run. The lead ballooned to 21 points with 6:49 left.

Once in the locker room, Johnson held the Big Ten trophy as a cooler of water was dumped on him.

"I know all outside noise is literally nonsense," he said. "It doesn't matter at all."

Not according to Lendeborg: "We put a lot of effort into this game, for the championship and for Rez. It means a lot to him, and it means a lot to us."

The next day, U-M announced that Cason, a spark plug off the bench and backup point guard, had torn his right ACL. He had scored in double figures four of his last five games. ▪

— *James Hawkins, Dave Eminian and Christian Romo contributed.*

Amid booing from Illinois students, Morez Johnson Jr. elevated above fan favorite David Mirkovic. RON JOHNSON/IMAGN IMAGES

JOHNSON JR.
21

MARCH 8, 2026 | ANN ARBOR, MICHIGAN

NO. 3 MICHIGAN 90, NO. 8 MICHIGAN STATE 80

STATE CHAMPS!

Wolverines sweep rivalry, show why it has the right stuff for a natty

By Shawn Windsor

They have more places to go than most teams in college basketball, and they showed it again in their regular-season finale.

Shut down their orchestrator and their rim protector? They will move to another part of the roster, and another part of the court, and it gives them their best chance at a Final Four and national title in a while.

This Michigan basketball team is clever and suffocating and relentless, and while Michigan State gave a good showing, the final result felt inevitable. That's how it is when a team can turn to so many places.

That's how it was against their rival, on senior day, as U-M beat MSU 90-80 to wrap up their best regular season in school history.

And on a day when their point guard scored two points. And their center scored four. It didn't matter. Not for this team, not with this depth.

Not with Yaxel Lendeborg, almost certainly the Big Ten player of the year. He scored 27 and hit five 3s.

Not with Morez Johnson Jr., who muscled his way to 18 points, including a 3-pointer dropped in because he can, tantalizing NBA scouts, no doubt.

Not with Roddy Gayle Jr., who doesn't need to score much, but almost always seems to find a basket or two when the game demands it. And finally, not with Trey McKenney, the true freshman guard who had scuffled the past few weeks, as so many freshmen do late in the regular season.

McKenney will be critical for a postseason run with backup point guard L.J. Cason out for the season with an ACL tear. McKenney, the 6-foot-4 Hal Schram Mr. Basketball Award winner from Orchard Lake St. Mary's, was U-M's most gifted player and surely would have a much bigger role next season.

This season?

He needed to defend, swing the ball and hit a few open shots when the swing pass came back his way.

He could get his own shot, and he showed that earlier in the season. That he didn't hunt for it on this day says as much about him as it did his coach, Dusty May, who had turned one of the most talented rosters in the country into one of the most unselfish.

"These guys are super teammates," May said, "which has made us a super team."

McKenney was a five-star recruit. He also knows he's surrounded by a handful of future pros, and he eventually will get his chance, as he did nearing midway through the second half Sunday, with U-M down four points and the atmosphere taut and anxious.

A coronation hadn't come yet for this dominant team. McKenney hit a corner 3 and pushed the ball on the next possession, drawing a foul and making

Roddy Gayle Jr. didn't panic despite a swam of green men trying to spoil his senior day. JUNFU HAN/DETROIT FREE PRESS

19
TENG
2
M

two free throws during an 11-0 run that gave U-M a 68-61 lead.

He wasn't the player of the game. Or even the second half. But his mini-burst helped swing the game, and he represented what made this team so good this season, and why they had beaten MSU twice.

Not to mention everyone else on their schedule — except for Wisconsin and Duke, and U-M may get a chance to avenge both in the coming weeks.

Still, 29-2 overall? And 19-1 in the Big Ten?

In Year 2 under May?

"This journey ... comes at you so fast," May said.

It had been a quick climb for May, and that couldn't sit well in East Lansing, where Tom Izzo rolled out a team arguably better this season than last year's Big Ten title squad and still came up a little short.

It's easy to think these matchups were a referendum on team building, but that's a disservice to both sides. May clearly developed his players and built chemistry. While Izzo clearly recruited, he just focused more on high schoolers than college transfers. Yet he had plucked critical pieces from other team's rosters in the past half-decade.

May, meanwhile, hit the portal this past offseason like Brad Holmes hit his first few drafts for the Detroit Lions. Four newbies — Lendeborg, Johnson, Elliot Cadeau and Aday Mara — helped give May the best locker room in the game.

Or at least one of the best.

"A player-led locker room," May said.

To hit on one transfer, let alone two, was difficult. But to find four? And blend them with a few holdovers and high schoolers?

That's why U-M would enter the NCAA Tournament as a favorite, if not THE favorite. That's why Sunday never quite felt as if MSU had enough, even though Jaxon Kohler and Carson Cooper and, yes, Jeremy Fears Jr. played the kind of ball that would give the Spartans a chance at a postseason run.

As long as Fears could find his way from the silliness; he kicked Cadeau in the groin in the first half after the guard was hugging him from behind and reaching around to swipe at the ball.

He was T'd up — again. And though he eventually found his equilibrium and pestered and frustrated U-M — mostly drawing fouls (and boos from the crowd), another cheap shot could end the Spartans' season.

As it was, the Spartan showed they were close to the best. Maybe on a neutral floor in a week — or two — they would show they were right there.

On Sunday, they showed they weren't quite. Michigan was. And had been for most of the season. And it showed again against the Spartans (25-6, 15-5 Big Ten).

The game-swinging run just came a little later than it so often had. Courtesy of a role player and a highly touted freshman and solidified by a couple of star transfers on an evening when the other transfers were a touch off.

It happened.

The Wolverines were built to overcome it. May made sure of that. ■

Finding a seam in the Michigan State defense, Morez Johnson Jr. battled for two of his 18 points. JUNFU HAN/DETROIT FREE PRESS

KOHLER
0
MICHIGAN
21
15
M
SPARTANS

THE GLORY

JUNFU HAN/DETROIT FREE PRESS

A DREAM TEAM

10 reasons behind Michigan's season for the ages

By Tony Garcia | March 12, 2026

As Michigan turned its focus to the postseason, it's worth praising the Wolverines' regular-season work one more time. A few of the milestones, as the third-ranked Wolverines:

- Won the most regular-season games (29) in program history.
- Became the first team in Big Ten history to win 19 games in conference play.
- Was the first team in 50 years (since 1975-76 Indiana) to go undefeated against league foes on the road (and the first to win 10 conference road games).
- Set a Big Ten record for victories by 40 points or more (seven).
- Still would have won the Big Ten outright if it *only* counted its games won by double figures.

Whew.

Now, Michigan headed to postseason play, opening its Big Ten tournament title defense on March 13 against Iowa or Ohio State in the quarterfinals.

But before then, let's take one more look at how the Wolverines secured the Big Ten's 1-seed, with the 10 reasons Michigan just put together its best regular season of all time.

1. Talent

Michigan put a loaded team together through a combination of the transfer portal, roster retention and the high school ranks.

The Wolverines' top five scorers this season weren't in maize and blue last year: Yaxel Lendeborg was the nation's top portal prospect coming out of UAB, Aday Mara was a five-star recruit in the class of 2023 before spending two seasons at UCLA, Morez Johnson Jr. was a four-star before his freshman season at Illinois, Elliot Cadeau was a former McDonald's All-American before spending two seasons at North Carolina and Trey McKenney was also a McDonald's All-American last season at Orchard Lake St. Mary's, where he won the Hal Schram Mr. Basketball Award as the top senior in Michigan.

Lendeborg went on to win Big Ten player of the year and make the All-Big Ten first team, while Johnson made the second team, Mara made the third team and McKenney was first-team All-Freshman in the conference.

That's not even including the bench, which featured yet another former McDonald's All-American in Nimari Burnett and a two-year starter at Ohio State in Roddy Gayle Jr.

2. Size

Michigan often overwhelmed opponents with its size. While its overall roster was No. 30 nationally in terms of average size (per KenPom), its starting lineup was simply massive. Mara stood 7-feet-3, Johnson plays bigger than his 6-9 frame and Lendeborg stands 6-9 and plays the wing.

Nine days after sewing up the Big Ten, Yaxel Lendeborg cut down a net after a victory over MSU. JUNFU HAN/DETROIT FREE PRESS

375lbs.
PODIUM
WERNER
2026
MEN'S BASKETBALL
CHAMPIONS
MICHIGAN
WOLVERINES
M

At Crisler Center after a 90-80 victory over Michigan State, the Wolverines celebrated their Big Ten regular-season championship on senior day. JUNFU HAN/ DETROIT FREE PRESS

B1G
CHAMPIONS
MEN'S BASKETBALL
2026
BURNETT
HAIL

U-M's starting frontcourt averaged 11.3 to 14.7 points and 6.9 to 7.4 rebounds apiece as the most balanced trio of bigs in the nation. But even beyond that, shooting guards Burnett and Gayle, at 6-5, were also bigger than average, while McKenney arrived in Ann Arbor built like an outside linebacker — 6-4 and 225 pounds at just 19 years old.

3. Depth

Talent was one thing, but having true depth was another. Michigan could beat opponents in multiple ways, rather than requiring massive games from one or two individuals.

Nine Wolverines in the rotation played 14 to 30 minutes a game, and of those, eight led the team in scoring at least once. Four of them did it at least three times: Lendeborg (11), Johnson (6), Cadeau (4) and Mara (3).

Burnett put up 31 against Penn State on Feb. 5 to set the team high — and he was the sixth-leading scorer on the season. L.J. Cason came off the bench to score 18 points while playing the final 15:15 at Northwestern on Feb. 11. Lendeborg topped 25 points in both victories over Michigan State. Johnson led the team with seven double-doubles (though Lendeborg wasn't far behind, with six).

4. Analytics

Michigan emphasized analytics this season, and it paid off with incredible efficiency.

Michigan was No. 4 in adjusted offensive efficiency (128.8) and No. 2 on defense (89.5), per KenPom, while ranking No. 10 in effective field goal shooting percentage (58.7%) and No. 1 in effective field goal defense (44.1%) — all while playing at the fastest tempo in the Big Ten on offense.

The Wolverines dominated inside, ranking No. 2 in 2-point shooting (61.6%) and No. 3 in 2-point defense (44.1%), in large part because of the proximity on those shots: Michigan was No. 23 in average distance attempted on 2s (4.8 feet) and was tops in the nation in keeping teams out of the paint, forcing opponents to shoot 2s from an average of 7.5 feet away, per KenPom.

5. Culture

Coach Dusty May has sounded like a broken record at times, reminding his team after nearly every game that it will make the Final Four only if each player is as happy for his teammates' success as he is his own.

Michigan makes a point for every player to stand with the player of the game in postgame on-court interviews; they pile towels on the head of the given night's star, cheer him on and bark like dogs. In recent days, they have made pizzas together, and some have posted a graphic on social media of their teammates' All-Big Ten selections before even posting their own.

"I think our guys are worried about the right stuff," assistant coach Justin Joyner said in October. "We have guys that are unselfish, guys that care about winning and guys that are really self-motivated. At the same time, we want to win and we want to do something special at the University of Michigan. I think those things can create greatness from within." (For next season, Joyner will be the head coach at Oregon State.)

6. Defensive dominance

Johnson, Lendeborg and Mara were selected to the Big Ten's All-Defensive first team, with Mara the school's first defensive player of the year since Gary Grant in 1988. Mara posted 2.4 blocks a game, thanks to 14 games with three blocks or more and at least one block in all 31 games so far.

Johnson and Lendeborg also averaged better than a block a game. Michigan finished No. 5 in block rate (15.9%). Plus, opponents didn't have much more success when shooting from beyond the arc, with the Wolverines ranked No. 7 in 3-point shooting percentage allowed (29.6%).

7. Offensive output

On top of one of the nation's best defenses, Michigan featured an explosive offense, topping 70 points 29 times; 80, 25 times; and 85, 19 times. That was fueled by two things: steadily improving on the offensive boards they finished No. 25 in the country in offensive rebounding rate (36.0%) — and 3-point shooting.

After struggling from 3 for much of January, U-M rediscovered its form to finish No. 41 in 3-point shooting (36.5%). Four Wolverines made at least 1½ 3s a game, and four of their five leaders in attempts shot at least 37.8%.

8. Road warriors

Michigan went 11-0 in true road games, including 10-0 in the Big Ten. That included some tough nights, with the Wolverines trailing in the second half in more than half of them.

Each time, Michigan answered. Their losses came at home, when Wisconsin made 15 3s, and on a neutral court in Washington to Duke, another favorite to win the NCAA title.

9. Never satisfied

May said it took "mental" endurance and stamina to survive the grind of the regular season; one way Michigan was able to do so was creating benchmarks for motivation along the way — starting with the Players Era Festival in Las Vegas during Thanksgiving week when Wolverines blew out legit teams three straight nights on national TV.

Later, the Wolverines found motivation for games against their teammates' former teams: Ohio State (for Gayle), UCLA (for Mara) and Illinois (for Johnson) were revenge opportunities, rather than Big Ten winter slogs. When Michigan visited MSU, it was about trying to get the program's first victory at Breslin Center in eight years. Against Purdue, it was avenging the worst loss of last season. Against Iowa, it was about finishing an undefeated road season. Then, in the finale against MSU, it was about the first regular-season sweep of the rivalry since 2013-14.

10. Coaching

May was voted the Big Ten coach of the year by media, which he then called the "staff and team of the year award." May, along with his staff — Joyner, Kyle Church, Mike Boynton Jr., Akeem Miskdeen, KT Harrell, Brandon Gilbert, Matt Aldred and Jacob Kohn — identified the talent that would take the team to the next level.

Church, the general manager, made sure the dollars made sense. Aldred, the strength coach, got the team in shape. Gilbert, the special assistant to May, had his hands on everything. Boynton was the defensive guru. Joyner was one of the most experienced assistants on staff. Kohn was the analytics specialist. Harrell was director of basketball ops. Miskdeen was intimately familiar with May, having worked with him on staff at Florida Atlanta from 2018-21.

The entire unit played a role in creating the best team in the Big Ten — and quite possibly the country. ■

PAIRINGS DAY

Despite loss to Purdue, U-M should feel good about road ahead

By Tony Garcia | March 15, 2026

Had anybody told Michigan before the season where it would wind up heading into NCAA Tournament — the No. 1 seed in the Midwest Region with Buffalo the farthest destination at any point in March Madness — it would have taken the deal in a heartbeat.

That perspective was difficult for players and coaches to find on pairings Sunday, however. Right before the announcement of the 68-team bracket, the Wolverines lost to Purdue 80-72 in the championship game of the Big Ten Tournament at Chicago's United Center.

Michigan had been favored to repeat as tournament champs and pull off a rare regular-season and tournament double. Purdue was the last do it — in 2023 — only to be stunned by 16th-seeded Fairleigh Dickson in its NCAA opener.

"We still feel like we're the best team in the country," point guard Elliot Cadeau said, "and we just got to do the stuff we did the whole regular season."

"We are the best defensive team in the country," forward Yaxel Lendeborg said, "and we didn't show that tonight."

Still, the 31-3 Wolverines received a No. 1 seed along with Duke (the overall top seed), Arizona and Florida. The Wolverines would play the first weekend at KeyBank Center in Buffalo. Should they keep winning, the second weekend would be back at the United Center and the final weekend at Lucas Oil Stadium in Indianapolis.

With their first-round game scheduled for Thursday — against Tuesday's First Four winner between 16-seeds Howard and UMBC — the Wolverines had no time to sulk.

Coach Dusty May said the team would have an off day Monday, practice Tuesday and travel to Western New York that evening. With U-M's opponent a mystery until the Wolverines arrived in Buffalo, the scout would look a little different. But U-M would prepare for the Bison and the Retrievers.

"We'll take a look at what both teams do and see if there's anything out of the ordinary we'll have to spend preparation time on," May said. "We just played three games in three days. ... There's going to be a lot of mental preparation, but it will give us a chance to clean up some of our stuff."

No matter which of the two advance, the Wolverines will be a 99% favorite. Assuming they move on, U-M would face 8-seed Georgia or 9-seed Saint Louis.

The Billikens, out of the Atlantic 10 Conference, would be the tougher draw of the two. Saint Louis was led by the burly and bespectacled Robbie Avila, who came to fame a couple years back at Indiana State with some of the best nicknames in the country, including "Cream Abdul-Jabbar" and "Larry Nerd." He led the Billikens in scoring at 12.9 points a game, but coach Josh Schertz's team was balanced, featuring six players who averaged between nine and 13 points.

The tests got tougher in the Sweet 16, with 4-seed Alabama or 5-seed Texas Tech looming. Alabama, led

Dusty May glumly walked off the court after an 80-72 loss to Purdue in the Big Ten Tournament final. JUNFU HAN/DETROIT FREE PRESS

M

by former Romulus High coach Nate Oats, had the No. 3 offense in the nation, per KenPom, turned the ball over just 13% (No. 4) and took 53.7% of its shots from 3-point range (the highest rate in the nation).

A victory in Chicago would set up an Elite Eight matchup against potentially 3-seed Virginia or 2-seed Iowa State. If chalk held in the Midwest, that meant the Cyclones — no doubt the hardest test in the region.

B1G season ends with a thud

Michigan didn't play its best over the weekend in Chicago, pushed to the limit in the quarterfinals by Ohio State (71-67) and in the semifinals by Wisconsin (68-65).

On Friday, Lendeborg, the conference player of the year, scored only six points, but his two free throws with six seconds left sewed up U-M's third victory over the Buckeyes.

On Saturday, the Wolverines squandered a 15-point lead in the second half when the Badgers went on a 23-4 run. U-M retook the lead with 45 seconds left on a 3-pointer by Cadeau, but Wisconsin's Nick Boyd answered with a 3-pointer with 29 seconds left. When a swing pass from Cadeau found Lendeborg on the right wing, he nailed a game-winning 3-pointer with 0.4 seconds left.

On Sunday, the Wolverines simply couldn't stop Purdue, which made 15 of 26 (57.7%) of its attempts in the second half and got 41 combined points from bigs Oscar Cluff and Trey Kaufman-Renn. Braden Smith, last season's Big Ten player of the year, was the reason. He got to his spots all afternoon, putting up 14 points and dishing out 11 assists. Of the Boilermakers' 30 baskets, Smith scored or assisted on 17 of them (56.7%).

"We can't let nobody come in here and punk us again," Lendeborg said. "We had that happen with Duke. (Purdue) did the same thing. They punked us down low and won the game. So, we've got to learn from that mistake."

That was more than enough to hand the Wolverines their first loss to a Big Ten foe in more than two months.

"It teaches you that you cannot relax in any game," center Aday Mara said. "Anyone here can beat you, you can beat anyone, so you've got to be ready for any game. ... We know what we're able to do. We think we can win it all."

There's no doubt Michigan can win it all. But it will need to play cleaner than it did to close out its Big Ten tournament rivals. Lendeborg needs to be aggressive, as he was in the second half against Purdue in scoring 13 of his 20 points.

Mara has to demand attention, even more than he did with 14 points and seven rebounds against the Boilermakers.

But perhaps most of all, the Wolverines will need their shooting to be on point. One off game can end even the most magical of seasons.

Michigan shot just 29.4% on 3s against Purdue, the second time in three games below 30%. The first weekend's foes may not challenge U-M's shooters, which could give May's group a chance to get its mojo back.

After that, the Wolverines will need to execute if they are going to cut down more nets in March and April.

"We'll take a step back and be very appreciative of where we are," May said. "But I would say it will be tomorrow until we can flush this loss. Typically, it's the day after we regroup and watch the film. ...

"We're excited to be playing. Just need to get back on the court and flush this." ■

After the loss to Purdue, Yaxel Lendeborg vowed that Michigan would learn for its mistakes. JUNFU HAN/DETROIT FREE PRESS

MICHIGAN
23

NCAA TOURNAMENT FIRST ROUND

MARCH 19, 2026 | BUFFALO, NEW YORK

NO. 1 MICHIGAN 101, NO. 16 HOWARD 80

'MARCH RODDY'

Right on schedule, Gayle's resurgence a good sign of the times

By Tony Garcia

Shortly after Roddy Gayle Jr. returned to the locker room, he removed his jersey and threw on his Trey McKenney graphic T-shirt.

A smile crept across his face.

He hadn't even been asked a full question, with only a prompt uttered — "Two words ..." to which he replied, "I already know what you're going to say."

"March Roddy," Gayle said with a laugh. "I've heard it over and over. Kind of leaned into it now, I mean, can't really escape it. Just kind of playing with that swagger, fearlessness, especially in March, the tourney."

Gayle scored 14 points in the Wolverines' 101-80 first-round victory over 16th-seeded Howard, third best for him this season. That included going 6-for-7 from the floor with a pair of 3-pointers — his first time making multiple 3s since hitting three while scoring a season-high 17 points against Auburn on Nov. 25.

To say his performance in the NCAA Tournament opener at KeyBank Center was expected might be going too far. But to say his teammates believed it was possible was an understatement. At the least, U-M's Yaxel Lendeborg saw it coming. Urged it on, even.

Lendeborg and Gayle had been fierce friends since Gayle was the future Big Ten player of the year's host on his visit as a prospective transfer last April.

Since then, the two had gone out to eat all over Ann Arbor — The Chophouse, The Earle, Mani, and generally with Trey McKenney as the third — and bonded off the court. That's why Lendeborg felt comfortable reminding Gayle of who he could be and who the team believed he was.

Lendeborg liked to play videos on the team's smartboard in its facility. His favorite, perhaps, was Michigan's 91-79 victory over Texas A&M in last year's NCAA Tournament — the origin of March Roddy, when Gayle came off the bench for 26 points (including four 3s) to send U-M into the Sweet 16.

"I've watched the Texas A&M game with him like four times, and we put it on in the locker room to tease him a little bit," Lendeborg said. "He has some Ohio State highlights, too, where he used to shoot hesi pull-ups and stuff like that, so I mean, just really excited to see how he performs come March.

"He talks about March Roddy and how he might have a downside in February, so I wanted to see the difference between those two guys."

Anybody have an extra ticket?

To do it in Buffalo, just 20 minutes from Niagara Falls, New York, where he grew up, was simply the cherry on top.

Buffalo wasn't exactly a desired destination for travel, Gayle said, so he knew all of his teammates

During a typical March effort, Roddy Gayle Jr. enjoyed the good times with Yaxel Lendeborg. JUNFU HAN/DETROIT FREE PRESS

GAYLE JR.
11
MICHIGAN
23

wouldn't use their allotted tickets. He hit up the team group chat after the draw was announced Sunday to see whether anybody had extras and they started pouring in.

Six here, five there, and in the end, he had 28 tickets to dole out to family, friends and former coaches.

"Pretty much anybody who had a hand in my development these past years," Gayle said. "I really just had my mom and dad handle all that. It was pretty much whoever's available and wanted to come, everybody come on."

Gayle has come off the bench the entire year, but against Howard (24-11), he didn't take long to heat up. Less than two minutes after he checked in, Gayle buried a 3 from the left corner to put Michigan up 11-4. He added a reverse layup moments later, then grabbed a loose ball under the bucket and put up a point-blank shot, then he laid in the ball on the next possession —nine quick points as Michigan led 24-17.

He didn't even attempt a shot again until the second half, when he nailed another 3-pointer in front of the Michigan bench. He looked back in their direction as his teammates stood and roared. Soon after, he swatted a ball at the rim.

Gayle has this in him, but with four seasons in the Big Ten — two with OSU, two with U-M — he's a fairly well-known commodity.

But for a team that only had four days to prep, he served as an unexpected right hook.

"He was playing defense; he was very efficient on offense," point guard Elliot Cadeau said. "Having a player like that coming off the bench, it's a look a lot of these teams we're playing haven't seen — someone that good coming off the bench.

"He would start on every other team in the country. ... We know we're down a man in L.J. Cason and it's something that we needed."

Deja vu all over again

Coach Dusty May wasn't one to believe that teams or players simply flipped a switch and suddenly improved. But he did believe in sweat equity.

It's why he never bailed on Gayle, even when he went 16 of 18 games without a 3.

"Yeah, he was awesome," May said. "His cutting in the first half, his rim pressure really helped us offensively. He shot great 3s, they looked good, shot it with confidence. I like March Roddy.

"Confidence, belief, situation, opportunity. ... The game usually rewards guys that keep showing up with great attitude and effort."

The star was Morez Johnson Jr., who scored 21 points, grabbed 10 rebounds and made all eight of his shots. The most unstoppable Wolverine was Aday Mara, who had 19 points, seven rebounds and six assists. They were in their first year with the program and had heard the jokes about March Roddy.

It's why Johnson wasn't surprised in the least that the senior guard had his most efficient game of the year.

"We knew," Johnson said. "We knew March King Roddy was coming back." ■

En route to 15 points on 5-for-6 shooting, Nimari Burnett threw one down against Howard. JUNFU HAN/DETROIT FREE PRESS

MICHIGAN
4
M
BISON
12
BISON
11

NCAA TOURNAMENT SECOND ROUND

MARCH 21, 2026 | BUFFALO, NEW YORK

NO. 1 MICHIGAN 95, NO. 9 SAINT LOUIS 72

SWEET 16 AGAIN

Wolverines shuffle off from Buffalo to Chicago's friendly confines

By Carlos Monarrez

Coach Dusty May didn't want to speak for his players.

Guard Nimari Burnett didn't want to disrespect his former teammates (he played for Alabama and Texas Tech before transferring to Michigan, schools the Wolverines could play next week).

But their slightly guarded answers spoke volumes about the big difference between this year's team, now headed to the Sweet 16 in the NCAA Tournament, and last year's team that made it to the Sweet 16 but no farther.

"I would say this year our guys expected to be here much more than last year," May said after a decisive 95-72 second-round victory over Saint Louis at KeyBank Center. "We were just in the fight, hoping to continue playing."

Burnett, a graduate student, said last year's group really came together during the tournament. This year's group didn't have to wait that long.

"I think the little bit of a difference," he said, "is we've just been so connected with this group this year all season long."

He listed pretty much every starter to key bench player as being part of that connection.

"I think with this group, our size, our length, our speed," Burnett said, "you combine that and we're going into Chicago, looking forward to the matchup and ready to come out with the win."

Before Elliot Cadeau and Yaxel Lendeborg, who were sitting next to him, could correct him, Burnett amended his statement.

"Two wins," he said.

Those victories would take Michigan from the United Center, where they open play Friday to Indianapolis for their first Final Four since 2018.

A more aggressive attitude

Of course, it's been obvious for most of this season that this version of the Wolverines was vastly better than last year's. That's why they're a No. 1 seed, after all.

The key to that success has been how well the team has come together with key transfers such as 7-foot-3 center Aday Mara, forward and Big Ten player of the year Yaxel Lendeborg, and elite guard Elliot Cadeau. That kind of talent and buy-in will do it for you.

That was underscored by the Wolverines' clinical dismantling of a very good 9-seed Saint Louis team that did its own 102-77 first-round dismantling of 8-seed Georgia.

Even when the Billikens went on a 15-3 run midway through the first half, Michigan answered with a 25-12 run to end the half with a 48-39 lead.

A Billiken didn't bother Yaxel Lendeborg on his way to a game-high 25 points. JUNFU HAN/DETROIT FREE PRESS

Wilson
MICHIGAN
23
OTENO
25

"There were several times that Saint Louis was on the verge," May said, "and we answered."

No disrespect to Saint Louis (29-6), but the Wolverines dominated the second half so well on both ends that it was like playing a little brother, letting him take the lead and then just taking it back. Sounds familiar for some reason.

Lendeborg, who had a game-high 25 points on 9-for-13 shooting and threw down one of the season's most thunderous dunks, was a big part of the Wolverines' improved aggressiveness against Saint Louis.

"We're going to start coming out more aggressively in the second half from now on," he said of the plan after failing to do so in the Big Ten Tournament loss to Purdue. "When they started going on their run, it went back to leaning on each other and playing poised and believing we can compete with anybody."

It also was evident in the Wolverines' defensive determination. Most notably, Mara put the clamps on Saint Louis center and nickname Hall-of-Famer Robbie "Cream Abdul-Jabbar" Avila, who had just nine points on 3-for-13 shooting — all on 3-pointers, when he was able to get away from Mara.

Long after the game, Mara was still beaming in the locker room, rightly proud of helping shut down the dynamic, burly, bespectacled focal point of the Billikens' offense.

"I was pretty excited because I saw his highlights, so the way he played, and I had like a lot of respect for him and for his game," Mara said. "And I guess, fun to watch him. He plays, he makes everything so easy, passes, 3s, he can do everything."

The Road to Indianapolis

I followed Michigan's NCAA Tournament run last year. Even though that team was good, this team was clearly much better in tangible and intangible ways. It's hard to imagine Michigan not reaching the Elite Eight or even the Final Four.

After all, last year Michigan came close as a 5-seed to upsetting No. 1 overall seed Auburn but fell 78-65 in the Sweet 16 in Atlanta, just 1½ hours away from its campus with a big home-court advantage.

Playing an opponent with home-court advantage was something May never considered until it happened.

"We went into this offseason thinking, man, if we could do our work throughout, we need to be better earlier, so we have a chance to earn some form of home court," he said. "We've earned the right to go to Chicago and hopefully pack that thing with Michigan fans and see where it goes."

Then he offered an honest assessment of where his program stood in Year 2 of his tenure.

"We're just a better team," he said. "We're better coaches. We're better players. That's just part of the growth process."

And yet another measure of growth for the Wolverines would be to get farther, if not much farther, than they did last year. ■

Nimari Burnett battled near the basket as Michigan secured a second straight Sweet 16 berth. JUNFU HAN/DETROIT FREE PRESS

4

MICHIGAN
NIKE

COACH

DUSTY MAY

Meet the coach whose secret sauce is how much he listens

By Mitch Albom | March 27, 2026

He is seemingly unflappable on the sidelines, his boyish face expressionless, his neatly cropped hair devoid of sweat. With his arms crossed and his jaw set, he could be a civil engineer overseeing a bridge build or a chairman of the board staring out his penthouse window.

So, it might stun you to learn that the day Michigan basketball coach Dusty May got his first head coaching job in college basketball, he cried.

Not out of joy. Quite the opposite. He thought he had made a terrible mistake. He had signed a contract with Florida Atlantic before getting a true look at its facilities or the existing team ("I'm a terrible businessman," he confesses) and once he did, he panicked.

"I remember it like yesterday," May says. "I went back to the hotel and realized it was too big of a job. There's no way I was going to build it. I thought I'd just committed career suicide."

May, to that point, had been the ultimate staff member. The guy who's never late, who works 120 hours a week, who finds no task too small, no request too unreasonable.

Such dedication let him rise from a student manager for Bob Knight at Indiana to assistant coaching gigs at Eastern Michigan, Murray State, UAB, Louisiana Tech and Florida.

"I was incredibly happy as an assistant at Florida," May says. "I thought we had a Final Four team coming back. Then to go into that (new situation) and feel like the world is collapsing around you because of what you didn't know."

He was 41. In charge. And over his head.

So, what turned him around?

"My wife. She gave me the tough love she always has. She said, 'You're not backing out of it now. You gave your word. So, let's get after it.'

"I started making recruiting calls about five minutes later."

You look at what Dusty May has accomplished since that moment in 2018, taking FAU — a glorified commuter school in posh Boca Raton, Florida — all the way to a Final Four and a 35-victory season, then landing with Michigan and turning an 8-24 team under Juwan Howard into a 27-10 record and a Sweet 16 spot in the NCAA Tournament in May's first year, followed by this year's Big Ten regular-season title, a top seed in the NCAAs and — so far — a 33-3 record heading into another Sweet 16 matchup against

Dusty May's first season in Ann Arbor saw him turn a 8-24 team into a Sweet 16 squad. He completed a transformation for the ages by earning a national championship in only his second year. JUNFU HAN/DETROIT FREE PRESS

4-seed Alabama, and you emerge from that hurricane of accomplishments with a single question:

How does he do it?

It's simple.

He listens.

Lessons from Bob Knight

Coaching, at many levels, can be a performative art. Especially in college basketball, where the players come and go so quickly that teams are identified coach-first. They are "Mike Krzyzewski's Duke Blue Devils," or "Rick Pitino's St. John's Red Storm."

It's easy, in such an environment, to become an audience to your own legend. Putting on a show. May, now 48, no doubt witnessed that working for Knight, who ultimately became so consumed by his own Patton-like persona that he overplayed it and got fired.

Like so many small-town kids in Indiana — he was raised in Greene County, about 30 miles from Bloomington, home of the Hoosiers — May grew up dreaming of playing for Knight. But when he peaked at 5-feet-10, he shifted his dreams from suiting up for the legend to studying him.

So much so that May walked away from his Division II college team at Oakland City University after one semester to become an unpaid student manager at Indiana. Playing ball was a joy, but coaching, he believed, was his calling.

"What did your friends say," he is asked, "when you gave up playing to be a student manager? You were only 18. Didn't they think it was cooler for your social life to be an athlete?"

"Well," he says, chuckling, "it was Indiana, I was a small-town guy, and Bobby Knight was like a god. So that was cool enough."

May learned a ton at Indiana, doing everything from breaking down tape to recording games, keeping statistics and mixing with players during drills.

But mostly what May learned is that working for Bob Knight didn't make him Bob Knight.

"I tried to be a mini-version of coach Knight when I started coaching at 19. And I realized after one summer that that wasn't the best way for me.

"I remember coaching an AAU game in Lexington, Kentucky, and we'd gotten up early and driven four hours, and I was a college student, I didn't have money, so we had to fundraise for the gas money and the typical stuff.

"We're playing poorly at halftime, and I'm literally screaming at them, 'Why did we do this? We spent this much on gas money! Why did we get up and do this? I did this! I did that!'

"And then I realized, they don't really care that you had to raise the gas money. I needed to separate myself out and find a way for them to be the best they could be. And it wasn't through screaming and intimidation.

"I didn't enjoy it. They didn't enjoy it."

And so, he went the other way. Instead of yelling, he focused on listening. And like Robert Frost's road less traveled, that has made all the difference.

A cultivator, not a commander

Consider the challenge facing May when he took over the Michigan job. The program was in the dumper. Only three players were returning. NIL money and the lightning-quick transfer portal — things that didn't exist when May started at FAU — were now determining factors in building a roster. And May was not exactly a magnetic household name, despite his Cinderella successes at FAU.

But one thing May had done his whole career was cultivate relationships. Someone who used to

Dusty May delivered a message to his Wolverines during the Big Ten Tournament in Chicago. JUNFU HAN/DETROIT FREE PRESS work with him. Someone he befriended or met at a clinic. Heck, during his interview for the U-M job, May reminded athletic director Warde Manuel that Warde's wife was the realtor who sold Dusty his first house in Ypsilanti in 2005.

That type of personal networking helped May bring transfer Vlad Goldin with him from FAU, despite many other schools chasing after the talented center. And forward Danny Wolf, upon leaving Yale, had some connections to U-M that May parlayed into his transfer to Ann Arbor.

Those two became star pillars of May's surprisingly successful inaugural run, as did transfers such as Roddy Gayle Jr. and Tre Donaldson, whom May circled in on and quickly closed.

"In the first year," May admits, "it was probably more the brand of Michigan that brought them in than me."

By the second year, that had flipped. Word got out about how May's teams played, how tight they were, how May was more a cultivator than a commander.

Plus, May and his staff were very clear about the type of player they were looking for. If you want to be "the man" at a program, stack your numbers, build your brand, parlay your stats into an NBA lottery spot, "then you shouldn't come here," he says.

That no doubt turned away some. But it attracted others.

"Believe it or not," May says, "I think there are a lot more players that want to play like that than most people realize."

In search of vulnerability

Still, selling a team concept in an ego-driven sports world isn't easy. May has managed to do it. Take Yaxel Lendeborg, who was considered the No. 1 transfer prospect in college basketball last year. He reportedly turned down an NIL deal in the $7 million to $9 million range from Kentucky to play for Michigan (at about half that amount).

And no, it's not the same as getting a player for free. We're still talking millions. But any time an athlete takes less money, there's a reason.

The reason in Ann Arbor is now the coach. Not just how he talks, but how he reacts when players talk.

"I've studied some of the best educators outside of sports," May says, "and I feel like when these guys are in a very stressful moment in a game, each situation needs something different. It might just be a hand on the shoulder to get them to relax and refocus, or it might need to be a sharp word to get them motivated or ticked off at me.

"Reading the situation and trying to figure out what makes each guy the best, being fair but being demanding without trying to bully them, that's what I want to achieve."

May offers the example of a new player during a film session last year who kept answering May's questions with what he thought the coach wanted to hear. May kept stopping him and saying, 'No, just tell me what you saw on this play, not what you think I want. I'm not trying to critique what you've done. I'm trying to understand how you see the game. Be brutally honest with what you saw and what you were thinking.

"I'm trying to get them to be very vulnerable with who they are and where they are. Then I can help them."

How many times do you hear "vulnerability" as a prime objective? Maybe in a therapist's office. Rarely on a basketball court.

Big stakes, better performance

But May's ears and patience have molded Michigan into a powerful unit now, one favored by many to make the Final Four and even to win it all. May, the married father of three sons, is well-liked in Ann Arbor. He's already had his contract reworked. He steers an even-keeled ship, values dignity and communication and gets along with the media. His players marvel at his ability to jump in and work out with them, on the court or in the weight room.

But in only his second year, it's the system he's developing that offers the biggest promise. Remember, this is a wholly different group than last year. Aday Mara is a transfer from UCLA. Morez Johnson Jr. transferred from Illinois. Lendeborg came from UAB. Trey McKenney was recruited out of high school in Michigan.

All four received Big Ten honors this season. We haven't even mentioned Elliot Cadeau, Nimari Burnett or Gayle.

It's the type of roster that can play a lot of different ways — smother you on defense, play over your heads with big men, drill you with fast play and high percentage shooting.

But to May, the best weapon is attitude.

"This team has a very businesslike approach," he says. "We didn't celebrate when we made the Sweet 16 this year. That was up to the players. They just felt like that was another step towards our ultimate goal."

In that way, they are mimicking their coach. That calm facade on the sidelines? That hard stare, but emotionless look?

It's deliberate.

"If I get too emotional over a call or effort, then I can't see what I need to be looking at next. I can't anticipate what they're doing. I don't feel like I can make the right suggestions to our guys, because I'm thinking with too much emotion."

And therein lies the secret sauce of what Dusty May has done in less than two full seasons. Take the emotional air out of where it doesn't belong (ego, player rivalries, anger over foul calls) and put it into where it does (listening, analyzing, advancing.)

"We're attacking this week just like we have the others," he says of the Midwest Region semifinals and final opening Friday. "It's not the NCAA Tournament, it's a small tournament in Chicago against Alabama and then either Tennessee or Iowa State, and we have to be prepared to play good basketball."

"But, I will say this about our guys." He pauses. "The bigger the stakes, the better they perform."

Going back to that panicked day in his hotel room — and seeing where May is today — you can say the same about him. ■

NCAA TOURNAMENT SWEET 16

MARCH 27, 2026 | CHICAGO, ILLINOIS

NO. 1 MICHIGAN 90, NO. 4 ALABAMA 77

A YAX ATTACK

Crimson Tide roiled by Lendeborg's 23 points, 12 rebounds, 7 assists

By Tony Garcia

In the big picture, Yaxel Lendeborg is the best player on the Michigan roster.

That's not to say the Wolverines can't win when he's not starring.

But when he does? When he puts up 23 points, 12 rebounds and seven assists, reaching benchmarks matched just two other times in the past 41 NCAA tournaments (by Carmelo Anthony and Dwyane Wade in 2003)?

Well, it tends to paper over his teammates' occasional individual struggles, such as, say, Morez Johnson Jr. and Aday Mara's combined 15 points (on 7-for-18 shooting), 13 rebounds and four turnovers in top-seeded Michigan's 90-77 victory over 4-seed Alabama for a spot in the Elite Eight.

Of course, getting big games from Elliot Cadeau (17 points, seven assists and one turnover), Roddy Gayle Jr. (16 points, one short of his season high) and Trey McKenney (17 on just seven shots) helps, too.

"Each game it's going to be someone else, someone different," Mara said. "We realized that today, the big men, our job was screen for Yax, screen for Elliot and they're going to create offense. So, we tried to do that as best we can."

But again, the Wolverines' Big Ten player of the year was the engine that drove the Wolverines' return to the Elite Eight for the ninth time in 42 seasons.

"We had about five guys not anywhere near their good stuff, let alone their best stuff," coach Dusty May told his team after the game. "That shows how capable we are."

'Just a lot of energy'

It wasn't all Lendeborg. Late in the first half at Chicago's United Center, Michigan began to pull away. Gayle buried a 3 from the corner. McKenney knocked one down from the left wing, then another from nearly the same spot as part of a 14-3 run that made it 47-41.

Gayle mean-mugged McKenney after the final one, and by the time the freshman was back on defense, he couldn't help but let out a roar.

"When you hit those 3s and get the crowd into it ... in the moment, you're just feeling it," McKenney said. "Just a lot of energy."

Gayle and McKenney combined for 33 points; Alabama's entire bench registered six. Cadeau completed the guard trio, with the Wolverines noticeably weaker, as May noted, when he had to sit in the first half with foul trouble.

With a final Alabama push before halftime, Michigan trailed 49-47 after 20 minutes. Then Lendeborg took over.

With 23 points against Alabama, Yaxel Lendeborg underscored why he was Big Ten player of the year. JUNFU HAN/DETROIT FREE PRESS

MICHIGAN WOLVERINES
MICHIGAN
23

'NBA player in college'

Lendeborg opened the second half with a step-back 3, simply shaking his head in silent celebration. Then he added a putback to extend the lead followed by a full-court outlet pass that hit Nimari Burnett in stride for a dunk.

"He loves those full-court passes," Burnett said. "As soon as I saw he got the ball, I was out. And it's like, if you throw a touchdown pass, I'm going to catch it."

That came after Lendeborg was on the receiving end of a full-court heave from Gayle — May called it a 30-70 ball that Lendeborg turned into a mismatch — to draw a foul and sink two free throws.

There wasn't much he didn't do: A bounce pass to Gayle on a baseline cut for a layup and three-point play. A 3 from the left wing after the Crimson Tide went under a screen. An aggressive drive and scooping finish in traffic after Alabama briefly got back within six points.

Does it surprise his teammates? Not entirely.

"I mean, no because I see it every day in practice," Mara said. "But at the same time, yes, because he's so dominant. I would say that he's an NBA player playing in college. The way he plays, the way he dominates every game, he does everything.

"He's playing full-court defense and, at the same time, making all the shots when he's playing offense."

After a season spent dominating with a three-big lineup, it wasn't working against the three-point attack from Alabama (25-10). So, May switched it up: McKenney tied a career high with 28 minutes, and Gayle's 27 was two shy of his high. Johnson's 24, meanwhile, were his fewest in the last 14 games.

In the biggest moments, Michigan (34-3) turned to its backup options — a choice made much easier by Lendeborg's dominance.

Now, U-M was on the brink of a Final Four, with a matchup against 6-seed Tennessee on Sunday afternoon, and three victories from the ultimate destination.

"We've felt like we had a team that can cut down the nets on the last Monday, and we haven't shied away from that," May said. "We've talked about it. Obviously, that comes with a different level of pressure and expectation, but I don't think that it's hindered us at all." ■

Trey McKenney (left) and Morez Johnson Jr. applied the heat to counteract Alabama's 3-point attack. JUNFU HAN/DETROIT FREE PRESS

Wilson
NCAA
ALABAMA
7
MICHIGAN
BIG

CAMP WOLVERINE

Foundation for magical season started with epic trip Up North

By Tony Garcia | March 29, 2026

With four players coming in via the transfer portal and a highly regarded freshman expected to play a big role, coach Dusty May knew he needed to bring his team together.

In the last week of August 2025, the Michigan Wolverines went Up North for an extended Labor Day weekend to a sprawling farm in Charlevoix. It belonged to Matt Lester, a big-time donor and founder of Champions Circle, Michigan's NIL collective.

The team rode ATVs, personal watercraft and boats, had family dinners and even roasted marshmallows around a campfire, taking their on-court connection into the wilderness.

The belief was that unity would come in handy when times got tough. That time now had arrived, with top-seeded Michigan set to face 6-seed Tennessee in the Elite Eight at Chicago's United Center.

"That was a super special trip," forward Will Tschetter recalled. "A lot of great bonding, getting to know one another off the court. Sometimes we're so caught up — we see each other at (the Player Development Center) every day or Crisler — so to be able to see people not touching a basketball, it really forces you to get to know them as people.

"That helps when things go south, things aren't going well. You can rely on: 'Man, I know you as a person, not a coworker or player. I know you as one of my friends.' ...

"I think that was one of the biggest things that helped us develop."

The Wolverines continued these sorts of exercises throughout the year, like a family-style "Jeopardy" game that featured personal questions about everybody during their two-game swing through the Pacific Northwest in January. But, as point guard Elliot Cadeau said, the foundation for it all was laid along the shoreline of Lake Michigan.

Tschetter had been in Ann Arbor for five years under two different regimes. He said none of the team-building exercises matched the Charlevoix trip. He called it a conscious effort by the coaching staff to make sure everybody got to know one another.

"I'd say just having 16 of us in a tiny bunkhouse was probably the highlight," he said with laugh. "We were like on cots, all over this house. It was definitely entertaining."

'Giant camp sleepover'

For star forward Yaxel Lendeborg, whose collegiate career began at an Arizona junior college and then continued at UAB, this was unlike anything he had done with a team before.

Gathered around the television watching Michigan play its football opener against New Mexico, he saw firsthand the passion that went into U-M athletics, even from players supporting other teams on campus.

The Wolverines toyed with coach Dusty May during an on-court interview after another victory. JUNFU HAN/DETROIT FREE PRESS

Even for other players who previously had extravagant trips, this felt different. Charlie May, Dusty's son, opened his career at Central Florida. His sophomore year, the team took an overseas trip to Italy.

That was longer and more extravagant, but this reminded him of his childhood.

"I don't even know how to explain this place," he said. "I mean, there was a weight room in there, a cold tub, it was almost like a giant spa. Then, in the basement, there were like four rooms and just like cots everywhere down there.

"It was like a giant camp sleepover. It was funny."

The activities were endless: A giant field that was like a driving range, spike ball, and, of course, cards while watching Michigan beat New Mexico, 34-17, at the Big House.

Once the fun outdoors ended, players started trickling in from the fire, to the cots, but that's when the NBA 2K games started, with some staying up until 5 a.m. gaming.

"So, it was some people trying to sleep, but then we had a bunch of dudes cracking jokes all night," Charlie May said. "There was a lot going on."

'A conscious effort'

There wasn't a player on U-M's roster who had reached a Final Four.

The holdovers from last year's team had made a Sweet 16, as had Cadeau at North Carolina in 2024. Lendeborg had played in one game in March Madness in his career while Aday Mara (UCLA) and Morez Johnson Jr. (Illinois) had never made it out of the first weekend.

The talent on Michigan's roster entering the season was undeniable, but that was only half the battle. Michigan still had to foster a culture of buy-in, built on the pillars of selflessness and camaraderie.

"There have been team building activities," Tschetter said, "but this was definitely a conscious effort to make sure our guys got to know each other."

Dusty May wanted to create bonds that would last a lifetime. It worked.

Lendeborg has said multiple times in recent months this had been the best year of his life. Mara has implied the same. Burnett, who has six years in college, says he never has played on a team like this previously.

Now, after a trip in August that started it all, May and company are on April's doorstep. ■

New Zealander Oscar Goodman (left) and Will Tschetter relished the Sweet 16 victory over Alabama. JUNFU HAN/DETROIT FREE PRESS

LOCK IT IN.
M
MICHIGAN
42

NCAA TOURNAMENT ELITE EIGHT

MARCH 29, 2026 | CHICAGO, ILLINOIS

NO. 1 MICHIGAN 95, NO. 6 TENNESSEE 62

ROAD TO INDY

After 21-0 run, U-M takes but a moment to celebrate Final Four berth

By Tony Garcia

There were hugs and high-fives, laughter and tears.

It was less than three minutes after Michigan finished ripping through Tennessee 95-62 in the Elite Eight at the United Center to advance to the national semifinals. There was celebration but also focus. This mixed reaction stemmed from a lesson the team was taught this offseason: When Dusty May was at Florida Atlantic, he told his team it needed to have March habits.

Only when he got to April did he realize there was another level.

So, from the moment the 2025-26 season began with offseason conditioning and summer workouts, May had the Wolverines eyeing April as theirs for the taking.

Hence, the reaction as the players hugged in line, yet hungered for something more.

"We got two left," Roddy Gayle Jr. said as he embraced a staffer who then echoed, "Two more, baby."

There will be time to analyze what's sure to be a heavyweight matchup between Midwest top-seeded Michigan out the Midwest Region and top-seeded Arizona out of the West Region scheduled for Lucas Oil Stadium in Indianapolis.

But this point in the journey deserved its own moment, even a brief one.

Will Tschetter certainly thought so. He was brought to tears as he held the regional championship trophy, teammates all waiting in line to hug the fifth-year veteran who had been through more than any other person in this program.

Not far behind him, Nimari Burnett, who came to Ann Arbor and then immediately endured the program's worst season in its modern era. Both could have left. But May felt their spirit and saw their work ethic as key pieces to what he promised anybody who would listen — fans, administrators, alumni — would be a quick turnaround.

That turnaround was complete. Michigan was back in the NCAA's final weekend, ready to show that although it might not be a historical blue blood — even if its ninth Final Four appearances were the eighth-most ever (and one more than Indiana) — it was a modern day behemoth, built for the moment ahead.

"From 8-24 to Final Four," Burnett said on the court. "There's going to be T-shirts with that someday."

'A dream come true'

The postgame scenes would live in photos for years to come.

Tschetter wore a massive Final Four banner as a cape when he walked up the ladder to cut off his piece of net. Elliot Cadeau, who conducted a masterful

Elliott Cadeau beat Tennessee's Ja'Kobi Gillespie for a layup during the Elite Eight at Chicago. JUNFU HAN/DETROIT FREE PRESS

MICHIGAN
3
TENNESSEE
0

performance from the offense in amassing 10 assists, wore the net around his neck. He liked it better, he said, than any jewelry he ever had put on.

When May walked up the steps to snip the final piece of twine, the thousands of Michigan fans who remained in the crowd erupted, chanting "DUS-TY! DUS-TY!" as he held up the symbol of U-M's hard work for all to see.

But the man of the hour was Yaxel Lendeborg, the top transfer who opted out of the NBA draft to return to college. All he did was average 25 points, 9.5 rebounds and 5.5 assists in two regional games to earn most outstanding player honors.

"I took a big risk coming back here; I worked super hard to get here," Lendeborg said, standing on the court while wearing his Final Four hat sideways. "Super happy this is possible. Super proud of these guys, too, man. I tried not to get emotional, but my mom gave me a hug and ruined everything I had going on.

"This is a dream come true."

He sparked the 21-0 run that turned a rock fight into a track meet: A reverse layup. A kickout for a Gayle 3, his own 3 from the left wing. The shots all built in a crescendo, the team as the conductor, the crowd as the chorus, roaring for the Wolverines and their beautiful music.

Michigan (35-3) trailed the Volunteers (25-12) by two points at 16-14 with 11:22 left in the first half. The Wolverines' epic run started 30 seconds later when Morez Johnson Jr. split a pair of free throws. When Elliot Cadeau hit Burnett for a layup with 6:10 left in the half, the Wolverines were ahead 35-16.

After Tennessee finally made a bucket, the Wolverines hit a free throw and scored a basket for a 38-18 lead. During Michigan's 24-2 run that lasted 6:12, the Vols missed 12 of 13 shots and turned the ball over four times.

Runs to the Final Four weren't supposed to be easy, but Michigan sure made it look that way. The Wolverines won their first four games of this NCAA Tournament by an average of 23 points, leading assistant coach Justin Joyner to agree on the court postgame that U-M was back at the level it played at while sweeping through the Players Era Festival in Las Vegas during Thanksgiving week.

Burnett admitted he was thinking exactly that midway through Sunday's game.

"It honestly was kind of reminiscent of that," he said. "I wasn't trying to tell that to my teammates and let it get to their head, but I definitely felt those vibes. I feel like this is a notch above (Vegas level), this is Chicago-level basketball."

'Not to be cliche ...'

Despite their locations scattered throughout U-M's locker room, Cadeau, Gayle and Tschetter unknowingly echoed one another when asked what the blowout victory meant.

Cadeau called it "a great accomplishment" before pointing out this was not the end of the road.

Gayle called it "a relief" that the Wolverines reached the Final Four, given the weight of the expectations they faced all season.

Tschetter walked from the postgame media table back into the room with his nameplate wedged into his shorts, the trophy tucked underneath his right arm. Two years ago, his odds of this moment "didn't look good," he said. Now, he could see his ultimate prize in sight.

"Obviously, we're super excited to make it there," he said. "We know that, not to be cliche, the job's really not finished. There's still two more games to play and two more times to put the jersey on."

Yaxel Lendeborg let out a primal scream after dunking on the Volunteers in a 33-point blowout. JUNFU HAN/DETROIT FREE PRESS

NCAA
B1G
MICHIGAN
23

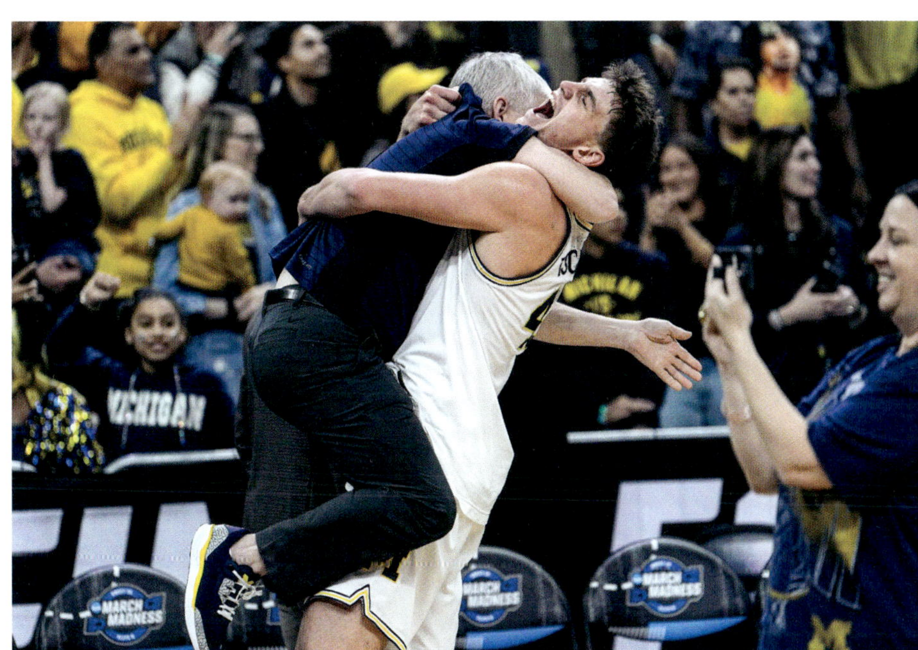

May changed his catchphrase from "March habits" to "April habits" for a reason. The Wolverines already were set to hang a piece of court, representing the Final Four in Indianapolis, on the walls of their Player Development Center in Ann Arbor. But to add the second national championship in U-M history would mean so much more.

The Wolverines grinded for this moment. It was telling that the roar for L.J. Cason — the guard injured just before this postseason run — was as loud as anybody else; the team sacrificed for one another since Day 1. It's all part of the buy-in to a formula to go from a talented summer group to one of the last standing in the spring.

"Daily growth," May explained. "This journey started back in June. If you're not getting better every day spiritually, mentally, physically — and sometimes there can be bad days mixed in — but as long as you're learning from that experience ... you'll be better for it. I think we've had a really strong growth mindset all year, never got too high, never got too low.

"This was one of our goals, but this wasn't the pinnacle for us. We still have work to do." ■

Opposite: Maize-and-blue confetti engulfed Dusty May, his players and their trophy. Above: Will Tschetter helped punch Michigan's ticket to the Final Four. JUNFU HAN/DETROIT FREE PRESS

FINAL
FOUR
SPORTS
RADIO
1290AM

CENTER

ADAY MARA

Michigan's big man from Spain owns a big dream to match

By Mitch Albom | April 3, 2026

This is the story of the first Spanish man to play in a Final Four and the very first thing he thought when he laid eyes on America:

"I was impressed," Aday Mara says, "with its size."

Wait. Isn't that what America thinks when it sees him?

Here is a college kid who has to duck under door frames, who, at 7-feet-3, layers pillows at the end of his bed so his legs won't dangle. Who, ever since he was a boy, has been buying two pairs of pants, cutting them in half, and sewing them together so they would reach his ankles.

Mara is a giant in every way — except the bad ones. No giant ego. No giant complex about his height. He is 87 inches worth of a smile just waiting to happen.

"What can I do about it?" he says, chuckling. "Cut my legs in half?"

Mara, whose expressive eyes, dark bangs and mustache suggest a 1966 Paul McCartney, is more than just 1) the most unique weapon on the Michigan basketball team; 2) the Big Ten defensive player of the year; 3) a shot-blocking machine; 4. an elite-level passer; and 5) an often unstoppable post presence.

He also 1) grew up amongst Roman ruins in a Spanish city that dates back to the 1st century BCE; 2) moved 6,000 miles away, without his family, to play college basketball in sunny Los Angeles; 3) left frustration there to find a home in much colder Ann Arbor, Michigan, and 4) was now two victories away from a national championship.

In other words, Aday Mara is that rare example of taking what nature gives you, and adjusting your nature accordingly.

'An A-plus human being'

Let's start with the height. An only child, Mara was destined to be tall. His father, Javier Mara, is a 6-7 ex-pro basketball player. His mother, "Gely" Gomez, is 6-3 and a former volleyball star. By the time Aday was in grade school, he was a head above all the other kids.

By the time he was 14, he'd reached 7 feet.

People around him, his father included, steered him toward basketball at a young age, but told him

With a father who played pro basketball and mother who played volleyball, Aday May was destined to be an athlete. His path to Ann Arbor included stops in Spanish professional leagues and two years on the bench at UCLA. JUNFU HAN/DETROIT FREE PRESS

ALABAMA
15

not to worry when "my body wasn't ready," and his long limbs made him slower or seemingly weaker than smaller, more coordinated kids.

"Your time will come," his parents assured him, a mantra he has lived by to this day. Aday made the Spanish professional leagues by the time he was 16, became the subject of a legal tussle between his pro team and UCLA when he was 18, rode the bench with the Bruins when he was 19 and 20, then transferred to Michigan last year to play for Dusty May.

Up to that point, "your time will come" was an annoying anthem. Although UCLA had promised a bigger role, it never arrived, and Mara, who began therapy to deal with the frustration, was starting to think promises were just tools coaches used to lure you.

But May was different, Mara says.

"He told me, 'I think you can be my starting center, and I think you can do great.' And he didn't change his mind. He didn't say one thing and do another."

May urged Mara to concentrate on two areas: his transition game up and down the court and being more physical. In a word, "meaner."

Which doesn't come easily to Mara. His default mode is kind, easygoing, funny, qualities that have led May to label him "an A-plus human being."

But sometimes, in major college basketball, you have to lose the Mr. Congeniality award.

"Most of the coaches that I had said the same thing," Mara admits. "That I'm always like, smiling. Sometimes they say that I'm goofy."

Is there a Spanish word for goofy, he is asked?

"Yeah, but it's not a good word," he says. "It sounds like a curse, you know?"

'It's hard to be mean'

Mara largely has shed that curse this season, rejecting shots a school-record 100 times, calling for the ball down low and elevating for hooks, layins or dunks. He has set career numbers for points (11.8), rebounds (6.8) and blocks (2.6) a game. He grabs motivation for physicality wherever he can.

"It's hard to be mean when nothing happens," he admits. "When something happens, and I get frustrated, I can be super mean. But that something has to happen."

He may find that something this weekend in Michigan's national semifinal against Arizona. The Wildcats likely will cover Mara with 7-foot-2 center Motiejus Krivas, a junior (like Aday) and a former international pro (like Aday) but a guy who is 40 pounds heavier.

Mara will have extra motivation. His parents will be in the stands in Indianapolis. Although they have visited a few times over the Christmas holidays, this will be the first time they get to see their son go for an American title.

"I told them we're gonna play in a football stadium that holds 80,000 people," Mara says. "They couldn't believe it."

College basketball has no parallel in Spain. Teenage talent is snapped up by club teams, national teams and professional squads. Mara admits he never saw a Final Four until last year.

"It's not big where I come from," he says. "It's getting bigger, though."

And, should he be cutting down the nets Monday night, it will no doubt skyrocket. Pau Gasol's success with the Lakers in the NBA propelled pro basketball to mass popularity in Spain. (Mara admits Gasol was a childhood idol.)

Now Aday has the chance to do the same for the college game.

Ready for a 'very cool' milestone

Still, what impresses most about this young man is his demeanor, his maturity and his apparent comfort in his own skin. He admits that people actually ask him, "How's the weather up there?" along with

Although a big man in the truest sense, Aday May possessed a nimble ability to pass the ball. JUNFU HAN/DETROIT FREE PRESS

NCAA
B1G
MICHIGAN
15

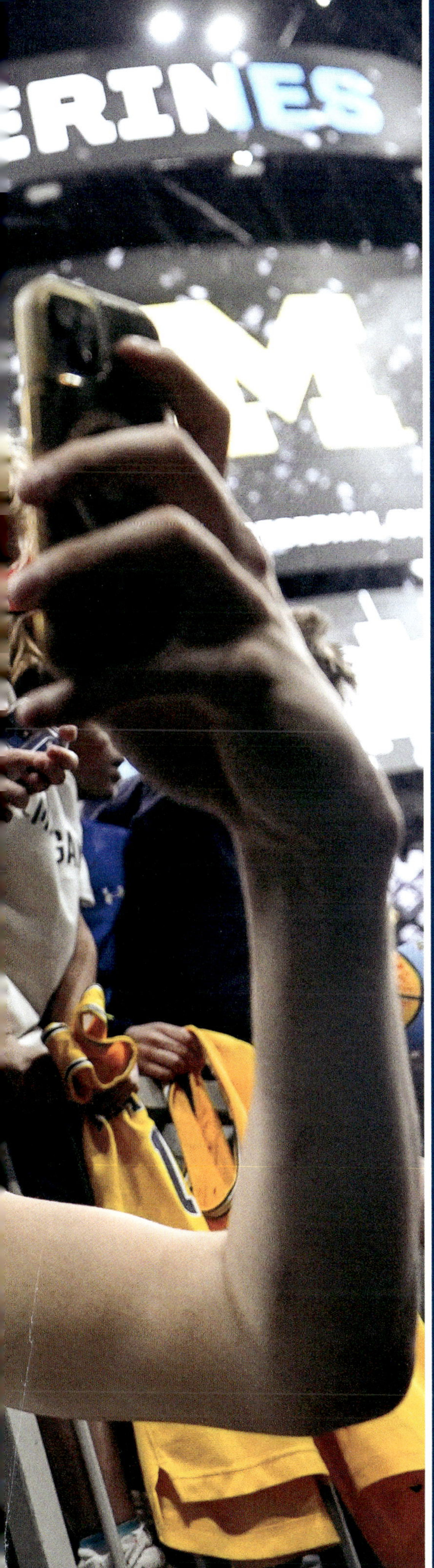

a handful of other cliches. But he never takes offense.

"As long as people are nice," he says, "I will be smiling and make the jokes. I get used to people staring. I can tell if they will right away. If we are in the airport, I will walk past someone and I will say to my teammates, 'That person will be turning to stare at me, turn around and look.' And they are."

He laughs. He likes to make a game out of things. He even empathizes with people's reactions. "It's hard to see a 7-footer every day, you know?" he says.

And while it's no joke that he cannot find a car to drive ("I hit the wheel with my knee, and then I hit that [console] thing with my leg, so I cannot hit the gas."), still he insists he would not trade his frame for a smaller one. He always wanted to be tall. And he knows it is a ticket to great opportunity. Mara will no doubt be a high NBA draft pick once he declares. He says he has not yet made his mind up about returning to U-M or going pro. ("Both options are good right now.")

But for this weekend, he is content making history, the first Spaniard to reach the men's Final Four and, should the Wolverines win it all, certainly the tallest player to ever claim a national championship for Michigan.

"I think in my head I can only imagine about 20% of what it will be like," he says, owing to the fact that this will be his first look at a national title. "But that 20% is very cool."

Hats off to a gentle giant who thought America was big when he got here and is on the lip of doing something awfully big himself. Life has been a series of adjustments, but to date, it seems, Mara has taken them all in stride. A long stride, perhaps. But — as he says — a very cool one. ■

A fan favorite, Aday May obliged young Michigan fans by snapping a selfie after the Wolverines advanced from their Chicago regional to the Final Four. JUNFU HAN/DETROIT FREE PRESS

NCAA TOURNAMENT NATIONAL SEMIFINALS

APRIL 4, 2026 | INDIANAPOLIS, INDIANA

NO. 1 MICHIGAN 91, NO. 1 ARIZONA 73

BRAISING ARIZONA

A victory beyond belief in spite of Lendeborg's fouls and pain

By Tony Garcia

The next-to-last game of the 2026 NCAA Tournament, with Michigan and Arizona squaring off on a Saturday night in Lucas Oil Stadium, had — on paper, at least — the makings of an all-time matchup.

Two of the top four teams in the past 30 seasons, per KenPom's rankings, going head-to-head in the Final Four, with a spot in the championship game on the line?

And then the Wolverines did their thing.

The top-seeded Wolverines took the lead 15 seconds in and then bulldozed their way to the final night of the season with a 91-73 dismantling of the top-seeded Wildcats. That set up a finale against Connecticut, a 71-62 winner over Illinois earlier and the No. 2 seed in the East Region.

UConn had won two of the past three NCAA titles. And yet, as Morez Johnson Jr. explained, as long as the Wolverines maintained the mentality they had against the Wildcats, the confetti that would drop from the rafters Monday in Indianapolis would be maize and blue.

"I don't know much about the KenPoms and all that other stuff, but we just came out and played our basketball," Johnson said. "What we've been doing all year — defending, getting stops, playing together, playing for one another.

"Me and Aday (Mara) knew they couldn't (expletive) with us, so we pretty much just came in and do what we do every game."

Indeed, Arizona did not, er, *(expletive)* with the Wolverines. Instead, Mara put up a career-high 26 points with nine rebounds, and Johnson contributed 10 points and seven boards. But the result in Michigan's ninth national semifinal appearance could have turned completely different.

For teams with less mental toughness, it almost assuredly would have.

Fouls and pain for Lendeborg

For starters, Yaxel Lendeborg picked up two fouls five seconds apart and headed to the bench 82 seconds after the opening tip. That, however, didn't stop U-M from opening with a 10-1 run. Minutes after he returned to the court, he tweaked his knee and reinjured an ankle while attempting a finger roll. He hit both free throws, then headed to the locker room. A 9-0 run got Arizona within five. That was about it for the competitive portion of the evening.

The Wolverines continued to find new ways to win without much from their biggest star — with contributions from big men, guards and reserves alike. Trey McKenney scored 16 points while banging home four 3s, Elliot Cadeau had 13 points and

Guard Roddy Gayle Jr. hung from the rim after a sweet dunk during a second-half onslaught. ERIC SEALS/DETROIT FREE PRESS

Wilson
11
10

10 assists, and veterans Nimari Burnett and Roddy Gayle Jr. combined for 15 points.

"It was impressive," coach Dusty May said. "But look, our superstars get too much credit, they do. Obviously, they're great players, but this has been a team all year. When you win at the level you do, you get the individual accolades.

"All our guys have had off nights and on those off nights, the other guys picked up the slack and that's the beauty of it all. No one's had to be at their best each night or we go home. ... The next guy's been ready to step up."

Lendeborg started the second half and finished with 11 points, thanks to three 3s, in just 14 minutes. He had a significant wrap on his left knee and had been scratched from some media obligations Sunday in order to spend more time with trainer Chris Williams.

But in the locker room, Lendeborg said he "absolutely" would play against the Huskies.

Even as Lendeborg's hoops contribution wasn't much in the big picture, the mental side of his return helped his teammates relax to open the second half. Michigan led by 16 points (48-32) at the time, and the lead reached 30 points (77-47) with 10:31 left in the game.

"With our depth, it allows us to pick up where he left off," Gayle said. "But especially after halftime — *just do it for Yax*. ... It's easy for a guy like that to just shut everything down and just look for his future.

"It's really good on your mind to know that he's OK ... just knowing he's tough enough to push through."

Arizona, a team built to protect the ball and punish opponents in the paint, nearly shot better from long distance than close range: 35.3% on 3-pointers (6-for-17) and 37% on 2-pointers (20-for-54). The teams turned it over at the same rate (14 UA, 13 U-M), but Michigan converted Arizona's turnovers into twice as many points (26-12).

Each team committed 19 fouls and had to sit players as a result. For Michigan (36-3), that included Lendeborg, Johnson, Mara, Cadeau and McKenney. Still, the Wolverines kept humming. The Wildcats struggled.

For Arizona (36-3), Jaden Bradley, orchestrator of the offense, only played 25 minutes and it showed during the other 15 minutes. He was the only Wildcat who was on the court for more UA points than U-M points (plus-1). He made 4 of 6 shots and scored 13 points, tied for the team lead with Brayden Burries, who missed 12 of 16 shots.

Winning any which way

As the Wolverines pulled within one victory of raising a national championship banner next to 1989's, they piled up NCAA milestones, thanks to piling up points.

With 2½ minutes left, the Wolverines reached the 90-point mark for the fifth time in five tournament games — the first team to score 90 points that often in a single postseason. They also were the first team to do so and win by double digits in every game.

That set up a secondary Monday matchup: Michigan vs. the history books. The Wolverines owned a combined margin of victory of 108 points in the tournament. Even a one-point victory Monday would land them ninth among NCAA champs. They were 32 points short of the record-holding champions, the 2023-24 Huskies.

And so, of course, there still was work to be done. UConn, despite arguably having less talent than its two championship squads this decade, was still 18-1 in the tournament over the past four years. To get to 19-1 for a third title in four seasons, the Huskies

Aday Mara threw down two of his career-high 26 points against the helpless Wildcats. ERIC SEALS/DETROIT FREE PRESS

MICHIGAN
15
Wilson
10

MICHIGAN
23
KRIVAS
13
ARIZONA
8

would have to down a Wolverines' juggernaut like theirs from two years earlier.

A trip to the Big House

On Saturday, U-M hit 12 of 27 3s in a stadium that supposedly punished shooters with its difference in depth perception. But the Wolverines practiced shooting in Michigan Stadium beforehand.

"Worst-case scenario," May said, "these guys went out and shot some hoops in the middle of the Big House."

It paid off, as so much had this season. The transfers. The returners. The recruits. The redshirts on the scout team. The assistants who stayed after May's successful first season. The messaging. The camaraderie.

This team that had proved it could win in any way just won its biggest game of the year in every way.

Thirty-six victories down, one to go, with one simple mentality, per Will Tschetter, who had been in maize and blue longer than anyone.

"Whatever it takes," Tschetter said. "Just win — win by any means necessary." ■

Opposite: Yaxel Lendeborg battled near the basket with Arizona big man Motiejus Krivas in the first half. Above: With Roddy Gayle Jr. (11) in hot pursuit, Krivas met the long arm of Aday Mara as he attempted to score from close range. ERIC SEALS/DETROIT FREE PRESS

IN FINAL FOUR, LENDEBORG RATES AS THE BEST PLAYER – AND TOUGHEST

By Nancy Armour | April 4, 2026

Yaxel Lendeborg kept it together, barely, as he limped away from the court in the first half. He had worked so hard. Come so far. And now he feared it was all over, his hopes for a national championship ruined by an injured left knee and once-again throbbing left ankle.

"As soon as I got in the tent, I started crying," Lendeborg said, his left knee heavily wrapped. "I definitely felt like I did all this for nothing in the moment. I definitely had to calm down for a little bit, speak with myself, get out of my thoughts.

"The training staff, they were being very nice to me, just being genuine, assuring me that I'm going to be OK."

OK? If Lendeborg isn't the best player in the country, he is for sure the toughest.

As his Michigan teammates got off a couple of final shots before halftime ended, Lendeborg returned to the court with a trainer. He walked on his tip toes. He ran the width of the court. He hopped on both feet. And when the second half began, Lendeborg was on the floor with the rest of the starters.

Despite spraining his left MCL and aggravating a left ankle injury from the Big Ten tournament, Lendeborg would play nine minutes in the second half. He made two 3-pointers in an 80-second span and grabbed two rebounds as Michigan routed fellow No.1 seed Arizona 91-73.

At one point, Lendeborg had more points (11) than minutes played (10).

"We know what type of guy Yaxel is. If he can play, he's going to play," Elliott Cadeau said. "He told us when he got on the court, he was going to give it his all."

As for the national title game, Lendeborg laughed when asked whether he would play. So long as he could walk, he said, he was playing.

"(The trainers) say they've got my back," he said. "They're going to make me feel good, and we're going to spend a lot of time together tomorrow and Monday before the game."

Michigan had scary depth — of the eight players in its main rotation, all but two had nine or more points against Arizona — but Lendeborg was what transformed the Wolverines from a good team into a great one. He was the Big Ten player of the year and a first-team All-American. He also was on the Big Ten's All-Defensive team.

A 6-foot-9 forward, Lendeborg was the basketball equivalent of a Swiss Army knife. He could score around the basket and make 3s from the logo. He could get rebounds and run the offense. He could shut down guards and big men.

He was unselfish, too. If Michigan needed him to score, he would do it. If one of his teammates was on a heater, he was happy to help make their spotlight.

"Yax is about winning," coach Dusty May said. "And from Day 1, he's always just been one of the guys." ■

Yaxel Lendeborg fought through early foul trouble and leg injuries to help Michigan advance. JUNFU HAN/DETROIT FREE PRESS

MICHIGAN
23
M
8

NCAA TOURNAMENT CHAMPIONSHIP GAME

APRIL 6, 2026 | INDIANAPOLIS, INDIANA

NO. 1 MICHIGAN 69, NO. 2 CONNECTICUT 63

LEADERS AND BEST

It's Wolverines' first natty since 1989, first for Big Ten since 2000

By Tony Garcia

Michigan basketball didn't need to shock the world, not this time.

It was a powerhouse all season, opening it with the goal of playing on the final night. It did exactly that and ended the year in glorious fashion, knocking off Connecticut 69-63 for the school's first national championship since 1989.

In the process, the Wolverines became the first Big Ten team since Michigan State in 2000 to win the Men's NCAA Tournament. And although only 2-6 in national championship games, the Wolverines became the 16th school to win at least two titles. They had lost four in a row (1992, 1993, 2013, 2018).

"Been coaching 25 years and there's nothing that's ever been anything like this that's resembled guys that have this much talent and given up everything for the team like this group," coach Dusty May said, his national championship hat backward on his head, moments after he cut down a net at Indianapolis' Lucas Oil Stadium. "We have a staff and a team that's going in the same direction all the time. We just figure out different solutions."

This one was far from an art form.

Yaxel Lendeborg, the All-America forward, said he was "really soft" and felt "awful" during a halftime interview, diminished by injuries to his left leg suffered against Arizona. It showed, as he scored 13 points on only 4-for-13 shooting, but he gutted through 36½ minutes, the most on his team by 6½ minutes.

Junior guard Elliot Cadeau scored 19 points for top-seeded Michigan (37-3), which was a 6½-point favorite after winning its first five tournament games by double digits. Cadeau, who had more steals than turnovers (2-1), was selected the most outstanding player.

Sophomore Morez Johnson Jr. posted a double-double — 12 points on 5 of 7 shooting and 10 rebounds.

McKenney's game-changing trey

Michigan lost the rebounding battle (46-39) as UConn grabbed 22 offensive rebounds.

The Wolverines came in eighth in the country in scoring at 87.8 points a game after recording 90 or more in their five NCAA Tournament games, a record. But against UConn (34-6), Michigan shot just 21-for-55 (38.2%) and was 2-for-15 from 3-point range, including an 0-for-5 from Lendeborg.

But the second 3-pointer couldn't have come at a better time.

UConn was down 62-56 and had a runout off a steal, but Solo Ball missed a contested layup. Michigan came barreling down on the other end, and a broken play led to senior Roddy Gayle Jr. slashing

Elliot Cadeau starred with 19 points against UConn and was voted the Final Four's most outstanding player. GRACE HOLLARS/INDYSTAR

MICHIGAN
3
FINAL FOUR
INDIANAPOLIS
B1G

from the left side and dishing to standout freshman and former Michigan Mr. Basketball Trey McKenney behind the arc from the right wing.

"Trey's step-back 3 to put the game away," Lendeborg said of what he would remember most, as he stood next to McKenney on top of piles of maize-and-blue confetti. "Just how hard we fought to get here, all those memories, all those strong men we did and all those early mornings."

McKenney caught it as a defender went for the steal, hit a gather dribble and stepped to his left before rising and burying the 3 to put Michigan up 65-56 with 1:50 left. The shot sent the Wolverines' faithful into pandemonium.

The battle was a stark reminder that champions weren't always a reflection of what they were at their best, but how they found a way, any way, to survive when they didn't have a crucial component of their recipe. Michigan went 25-for-28 at the foul line (89.3%).

The Wolverines never landed a major punch but used a 6-0 run late in the first half and a 10-4 run early in the second half as the turning points to turn a two-point deficit into an 11-point lead.

The Huskies got as close as 67-63 with 37 seconds left but never over the hump. U-M's length disrupted UConn shooters all night long. The Huskies entered making 56.7% of its 2s, yet shot just 34.3% on such attempts.

UConn had a chance after Gayle missed two free throws with 25 seconds left, but senior forward Alex Karaban barely nicked the front rim on a 3-pointer. McKenney battled for the rebound, was fouled with 13.4 seconds to play and made both free throws.

Karaban led 2-seed UConn with 17 points. The Huskies suffered their first loss in an NCAA championship game — in seven tries — and were unable to win their third title in four years.

Slowly pulling away

Michigan's No. 1 rated defense won the game by challenging shots and blocking six of them. UConn shot 30.9% (21-for-68) but battled for 22 offensive rebounds, seven from Michigan transfer Tarris Reed Jr. (13 points, 14 rebounds).

The Wolverines turned up their defensive intensity coming out of the half, forcing four UConn turnovers in less than four minutes.

The Wolverines weren't exactly explosive, going 2-for-6 during the stretch with three turnovers, but after Cadeau hit an and-one layup (drawing Ball's fourth foul) and Lendeborg followed with one of his own, U-M's lead grew to 41-33.

After McKenney hit the first shot outside the paint — a midrange jumper behind the free throw line — Cadeau followed with a layup and then a deep 3 from the left wing to put Michigan up 48-37 with 12:56 left, the crowd rising.

Slowly, UConn chipped away. The Huskies were within five and coach Dan Hurley was jumping around and pumping up the UConn fans when Nimari Burnett deflected an entry pass which led to a runout by Gayle, who threw it up near the rim for junior Aday Mara to come flying in and slam it home.

Michigan appeared to put the game away with McKenney's 3 from the right side, but UConn had one last push.

"I feel like we got it done for the university," Gayle said. "Now, just kind of waiting for that parade." ■

Aday Mara tipped the shot of UConn forward Tarris Reed Jr. as Michigan turned up its defensive intensity. GRACE HOLLARS/INDYSTAR

15
REED JR
5

IN ONE SEASON, LENDEBORG LEAVES A LEGACY FOR ALL WHO FOLLOW

By Tony Garcia | April 6, 2026

Cazzie Russell. Rudy Tomjanovich. Glen Rice. Trey Burke. The Fab Five.

And now?

Yaxel Lendeborg.

Although his time in Ann Arbor wasn't quite one calendar year, his impact on Michigan basketball will go down with the same reverence afforded to the Wolverines' all-time greats. The graduate transfer who took a chance on coach Dusty May to withdraw his name from the NBA draft and play an extra season of college basketball got the biggest reward imaginable, when Michigan defeated Connecticut 69-63 for the national championship at Lucas Oil Stadium.

"Best decision I ever made," Lendeborg said, his arm around freshman teammate Trey McKenney on a court covered in maize-and-blue confetti. "This is the best year of my life. I've said that many times. ... I'm just super grateful to be here."

Lendeborg completed everything he set out to do at Michigan.

The Wolverines (37-3) won more games this season than in any other in program history. They went 19-1 in the Big Ten, setting a record for single-season victories in conference play en route to a four-game edge in the standings. That included a record 10-0 mark on the road in Big Ten play. Now, they were national champions, bringing the title home to Ann Arbor for just the second time in 109 seasons.

Those within the program — players, coaches, trainers and staffers — pass credit around to many, but truly, after May, Lendeborg made it happen. He arrived a superstar — paid millions to wear the maize and blue— but never made it about himself. He reveled in his teammates' success, even as he had to learn to be The Guy.

For one of his teammates, it started with their first meal together, at The Brown Jug in Ann Arbor last spring.

"You just meet people you get around, you can just tell that he had an unselfish nature about him," Nimari Burnett said. "Every single moment that we spend around him, he was so humble, you know, kind of in a way, like diminishing himself to be about the team.

"He improved our chemistry, just about, like, being a person that he is, but also just (upped) our togetherness because of his unselfish nature."

When Lendeborg suffered a bone bruise and sprained both his ACL and ankle in the victory over Arizona, he could have taken it easy.

His mother and agent wanted him to. They had been with him for years and knew he was just a few months away from getting an eight-figure payday in the NBA draft, likely as a lottery pick.

But he refused to bail on his team, not with history on the line. In his final act of selflessness, he ran the risk of further injury — though imaging tests came

Despite ACL and ankle sprains, Yaxel Lendeborg played the most minutes of any Wolverine. JUNFU HAN/DETROIT FREE PRESS

MICHIGAN
23
HUSKIES

back clean — to give everything he had left. He never put a percentage on it, even when trainer Chris Williams asked, but Williams said later that he thought Lendeborg was, at best, operating at 70%.

"Everything that we became, started with him," assistant coach Mike Boynton Jr. said. "It was never a thought that he would not play in this game ever. If today — I believe this — if somebody said you could play tonight and the rest of your career would be over, he would have played tonight."

Monday was far from his best night, as Lendeborg would readily admit. He made just 4 of 13 shots, missed all five of his 3-pointers and tied season lows in rebounds (two) and assists (one). Yet he gutted and grinded through 36½ minutes — more than he played in all but three games all year — despite extreme discomfort.

Each of his 13 points, however, was huge. He got on the board with a pair of free throws midway through the first half, then finally hit his first shot, a glasser on the left block to give Michigan a 27-25 lead as part of a four-point possession with 3:06 left in the first half.

In the second half, with Michigan up nine points, he scored six straight for the Wolverines in 91 seconds, answering a pair of Braylon Mullins 3s as the Huskies tried to claw back into the game.

"We're extremely proud to be a part of the Yaxel's journey," May said. "Obviously, it's not a normal route that he took, but he's grown so much, and he's given us. He gave us so much because he was all about the team. Even though the individual accolades as his performance increased, he stayed more committed to the team."

As the players and coaches hugged, cried, posed for pictures, played music and celebrated in the locker room, there was a bittersweet feeling in the air.

It was one of the first things out of May's mouth, as he acknowledged a sadness knowing this group would never be together again.

How will Lendeborg be remembered? It was just one year, yes, but he led the program to its first national title since 1989. Rice was the face of that team, and his jersey hung in the rafters at Crisler, as did the jerseys of Burke and Russell. They, of course, couldn't quite lift the Wolverines to the top.

Lendeborg could.

And so, the question for May on Monday night, after the Wolverines' victory answered nearly all the others, was whether Lendeborg was one of Michigan's all-time greats?

"I don't determine it, but I don't know how he couldn't," May said. "He's an All-American and a national champion."

In the end, as he demonstrated he was The Guy, perhaps what Lendeborg will feel best about is how he will be remembered by his teammates as just another one of the guys. ■

Paying homage to the 1989 Wolverines, Yaxel Lendeborg relished Michigan's second championship. JUNFU HAN/DETROIT FREE PRESS

SHOCK THE WORLD
BOYS
GO BLUE !
TOL
BONUS

JUNFU HAN/DETROIT FREE PRESS